Diversity Dysfunction

The DEI Threat to National Security Intelligence

John A. Gentry

Diversity Dysfunction

The DEI Threat to National Security Intelligence

John A. Gentry

Academica Press
Washington~London

Library of Congress Cataloging-in-Publication Data

Names: Gentry, John A. (author)
Title: Diversity dysfunction : the dei threat to national security
intelligence | Gentry, John A.
Description: Washington : Academica Press, 2025. | Includes references.
Identifiers: LCCN 2024946069 | ISBN 9781680535631 (hardcover) |
9781680535655 (paperback) | 9781680535648 (e-book)

Contents

Preface

The emergence of "diversity, equity, and inclusion" (DEI) policies in the U.S. federal government during Barack Obama's administration has been as controversial as similar concepts have been in American universities and businesses. Claims that DEI policies are ethically good and necessary to redress historical injustices largely reflect ideological beliefs with which people can agree or disagree. But now, claims that DEI policies improve the operational performance of institutions have been met by equally strenuous claims – and a rising body of empirical evidence – suggesting that such policies are themselves discriminatory and damage institutions into which they are injected. It is important to test such claims.

My focus on this subject began after it became clear to me that DEI policies—and the ideological beliefs they reflect and material advantages they offer—were major causes of the eruption of overt politicization of the intelligence community (IC), especially the Central Intelligence Agency (CIA), in 2016 and thereafter in opposition to candidate and then President Donald J. Trump. I experienced politicization of a minor sort in the mid-1980s, when I was a CIA analyst. I studied the phenomenon in the United States and elsewhere thereafter and have since been sensitive to the subject as I became aware of the damage that any form of politicization can do to any intelligence service and the decision-making processes that intelligence supports. Soon after the first overtly political action against Trump—former deputy CIA director Michael Morell's op-ed in the *New York Times* on August 5, 2016—I began to write on the politicization of intelligence and quickly concluded that DEI was its prime motivator. I also wrote an article, "Demographic Diversity in U.S. Intelligence Personnel: Is It Functionally Useful?" (*International Journal of Intelligence and CounterIntelligence* 36:2 (2021)), which assessed claims that DEI policies improved the performance of U.S. intelligence and concluded that they were unfounded. When I proposed to two university presses my eventually published book on the politicization of intelligence, *Neutering the CIA: Why US Intelligence Versus Trump Has Long-Term Consequences* (Armin Lear, 2023), they rejected my proposal explicitly due to my assessment of the role of DEI policies. They appeared to have formed hard, ideologically driven views of the subject and were unreceptive to any discussion of the subject. My initial article on the subject also began a process that led Georgetown University to "cancel" my appointment as an adjunct professor in 2023.

Hence, this subject is fraught with many varieties of politics, as well as emotion and sometimes harsh actions. But it is an important issue to understand fully. After a balanced inquiry—in the sense that I brought no predetermined conclusions to my investigation—I have become convinced that DEI policies are harming U.S. national security, and the security of allies whose governments also embrace them in various forms. This book is my dispassionate effort to describe why, hampered as I am by the objectively Marxist nature of DEI, which makes all discussion of this matter inherently political.

This book is made possible by the willingness of many current and former intelligence officers to talk about a subject that is bureaucratically and politically dangerous to discuss, as I experienced myself. While there is some relevant material in the public domain, current and former intelligence officers really know what has happened and what continues to happen in their agencies. Many sources cited herein, including retired officers, were only willing to talk anonymously for fear of consequences that a strikingly large number perceived independently of each other. I therefore am grateful to all of these people, especially to those who were willing to be named.

I also am grateful to people who helped make this book a reality. Chuck Burgess introduced me to Dr. Paul du Quenoy of Academica Press, who appreciated my story and helped make it public. At Academica, Soumyadev Bose was a helpful project editor. Thanks to all.

This book contains a few passages taken with permission and minor modifications from some of my previous publications, including the article and book mentioned above.

As a former intelligence officer, I am required to submit my writings to government security reviewers before they are published. This book was reviewed by the CIA's Prepublication Classification Review Board (PCRB), which approved its text with minor changes. The PCRB requires the following statement:

> *All statement of fact, opinion, or analysis expressed are those of the author and do not reflect the official positions or views of the Central Intelligence Agency (CIA) or any other U.S. Government agency. Nothing in the contents should be construed as asserting or implying U.S. Government authentication of information or CIA endorsement of the author's views. This material has been reviewed by the CIA to prevent the disclosure of classified information. This does not constitute an official release of CIA information.*

Chapter 1

Introduction

Variants of "diversity, equity, and inclusion" (DEI) policies have become popular in Western governments, educational institutions, and businesses in recent years. These have been touted primarily as ethically (and politically) desirable policies. But many adherents, following a series of prominent McKinsey & Company reports that have recently been called into question,[1] have claimed that DEI policies in general are operationally effective in a wide variety of settings. McKinsey's assertions were backed primarily by studies that associate DEI policies with excellent domestic American business performance, especially firms' profitability measures. These findings typically are based on large-scale statistical studies that find *correlations* between demographically diverse work forces or leadership demographics, especially of corporate boards of publicly held American companies, and profitability measures, but rarely establish *causality* resulting from DEI policies. These claims also have been challenged on statistical grounds.[2] Adherents of popular studies that extol the virtues of DEI policies typically ignore these challenges, however, and assume that the correlations reflect causality despite the lack of direct evidence. Thus, a core implicit, and sometimes explicit, assertion of DEI advocates is that favored demographic groups have distinctive intellectual or behavioral characteristics at the group level that inherently only

---

[1] For example, Vivian Hunt, Dennis Layton, and Sara Prince, "Diversity Matters," McKinsey & Co., February 2, 2015, https://www.mckinsey.com/~/media/mckinsey/business%20functions/people%20and%20organizational%20performance/our%20insights/why%20diversity%20matters/diversity%20matters.pdf.

[2] Jeremiah Green and John R. M. Hand, "McKinsey's Diversity Matters / Delivers / Wins Results Revisited," *Econ Journal Watch* 21:1 (2024): 5-34; James Mackintosh, "Diversity Was Supposed to Make Us Rich. Not So Much," *Wall Street Journal*, June 29-30, 2024, B5.

improve institutions' operational performance. This highly contested assertion is almost certainly wrong.

Also commonly cited is a study by the late Professor Katherine Phillips of Columbia University's Business School, a black academic, and her colleagues.[3] Phillips et al.'s study noted that "social diversity in a group can cause discomfort, rougher interactions, a lack of trust, greater perceived interpersonal conflict, lower communication, less cohesion, more concern about disrespect, and other problems."[4] But still, the team asserted, diversity is good because racially diverse groups allegedly think better than racially homogenous groups because group members feel a need to perform better against outside groups. The analysis was based on the obviously subjective belief that "being with similar others leads us to think we all hold the same information and share the same perspective."[5] Phillips's team, like McKinsey's and others, identified some domestic situations in which greater race and gender diversity are *associated* with better performance. For example, the Phillips team found that a minority person on a team of three undergraduate students in American colleges was *associated* with better ability of the teams to solve murder mysteries.[6] Why this example was chosen to explain business decision-making is unclear.[7]

The attractive assertion—to DEI partisans—that demographic diversity improves performance was soon followed by similar claims by senior U.S. intelligence officers who reified Phillips's hypothesis into causal logic and extended it to foreign intelligence activities—thereby making Phillips's argument ostensibly relevant to the U.S. intelligence community (IC). Director of national intelligence (DNI) James Clapper

---

[3] Katherine W. Phillips, et al., "How Diversity Works," *Scientific American* 311:4 (2014): 42–47.

[4] Ibid., 45-46.

[5] Ibid., 45.

[6] Ibid.

[7] Implicitly Phillips's group argued that minorities understand murder better, which is perhaps accurate given that black Americans people commit murder, and are victims of murder, at much higher rates than all other major US demographic groups. See FBI murder statistics for 2016, crime statistics https://ucr.fbi.gov/crime-in-the-u.s/2016/crime-in-the-u.s.-2016/tables/expanded-homicide-data-table-3.xls. See also https://www.bjs.gov/content/pub/pdf/htius.pdf.

(2010-2017) asserted that DEI policies *cause* improvement in the operational performance of intelligence services. He said, for example, that it was "advantageous to employ openly transgender employees, who brought unique perspectives to mission challenges and contributed to successes."[8] Clapper did not describe or explain *how* these "unique perspectives" might help analysts, logisticians, linguists, information technology personnel, or individuals in any other functional intelligence job category perform their work. He did not argue, like Phillips, that transgender people would be helpful because they competed against cisgendered "others." But he undercut his argument by recognizing that a major cause of the increased hiring of LGBTQ+ people in his years as DNI arose not from talent, ability, or results, but from "tremendous outside pressure from LGBT groups that were seasoned from fighting for gay, lesbian, and bisexual Americans' rights and had embraced transgender rights as the next battlefield."[9]

Former deputy chief of the Central Intelligence Agency's (CIA's) analysis directorate Carmen Medina, a Puerto Rican woman, borrowed extensively from Phillips's argument in claiming that demographic diversity in groups following the same intelligence issue makes people work harder to prepare their arguments, thereby allegedly making them perform better.[10] Medina's argument that diversity encourages intelligence analysts to think harder is unpersuasive for several reasons beyond the weaknesses of Phillips's argument. For example, intelligence analysts are drilled constantly on the importance of thorough work—independent of the presence of any demographic "other." The sometimes lengthy coordination and review processes of all IC analytic organizations, often performed by floating groups of many analysts and managers with appreciably different intellectual and demographic backgrounds, have long been designed to help ensure the completeness of analysis and absence of bias in analytic products caused by all sources, including intra-

---

[8] James R. Clapper with Trey Brown, *Facts and Fears: Hard Truths from a Life in Intelligence* (New York: Viking, 2018), 301.

[9] Ibid.

[10] Carmen Medina, "Want a Sharper, Stronger CIA? Hire Folks Who Look Like America," *Overt Action*, March 24, 2016, http://www.overtaction.org/2016/03/want-a-sharper-stronger-cia-hire-folks-who-look-like-america/.

office competition with demographic "others." They have done so with incomplete success but generated strong bureaucratic incentives for good work.[11] Rapid progress through the review process is well-known to be career-enhancing—a far more powerful incentive to do good work than possible, but not inevitable, competition with demographic "others." Moreover, despite increases in team projects in recent years, analysts still generally work alone and are competitive with other analysts for promotion and plum assignments, meaning Medina's argument is often irrelevant.[12] Well-recognized errors caused by cognitive biases cannot be addressed by demographic diversity; only intellectual preparation, self-awareness, and diverse educations and experiences can help.[13] In addition, because the Office of Analytic Integrity and Standards of the Office of the Director of National Intelligence (ODNI), which reviews some analytic papers' quality and reports on them to Congress, purposefully does not assess the accuracy of analyses, there is no way the IC can test Medina's assertions with any degree of methodological rigor.[14] As a former senior CIA officer, Medina presumably knew this.

Hence, strikingly given long-standing U.S. intelligence norms and policy that require that evidence supports intelligence analyses to the extent possible, no U.S. intelligence officer has ever explained how domestically defined demographic, not intellectual, diversity improves the performance of U.S. intelligence agencies or the IC as a whole.[15] They have not provided evidentiary support or even vaguely suggestive anecdotes to back this claim. Nobody has ever credibly attributed even one significant intelligence failure to a dearth of demographic diversity, and history is filled with cases of successful intelligence operations conducted

---

[11] John A. Gentry, "Managers of Analysts: The Other Half of Intelligence Analysis," *Intelligence and National Security* 31:2 (2016): 160-163.

[12] For example, Anonymous, "The DI's Organizational Culture," 21-25.

[13] John A. Gentry, "The 'Professionalization' of Intelligence Analysis: A Skeptical Perspective," *International Journal of Intelligence and CounterIntelligence* 29:4 (2016): 658, 665-666.

[14] John A. Gentry, "Has the ODNI Improved U.S. Intelligence Analysis?" *International Journal of Intelligence and CounterIntelligence* 28:4 (2015): 644-645.

[15] Intelligence Community Directive 203, "Analytic Standards," 2022, https://www.dni.gov/files/documents/ICD/ICD-203_TA_Analytic_Standards_21_Dec _2022.pdf.

virtually exclusively by white men. For example, one of the finest intelligence operations of all time, the intelligence-enabled deception that convinced Hitler and the German military that the Western allies' invasion of France would occur in the Pas-de-Calais region of northern France and not Normandy in 1944, was conducted virtually entirely by white British men from a wide range of personal, cultural, and professional backgrounds who were drawn together by the existential threat posed to Britain by Hitler's Germany.[16] These important points said, it is crystal clear that capable people of all demographic groups can be, and are, effective intelligence officers. But DEI ideology defines demographic identity group, not individual people, as the unit of analysis in such discussions.

In 2021, I examined the DEI-related performance claims by Clapper and others, finding no evidence to support their assertions.[17] The longstanding argument that the skills of individuals, not groups of any sort, make good intelligence officers remains valid. I suggested that a follow-on study examine a related question: do DEI policies affect the IC's operational performance in any way? Reaction to this study was strong. DEI advocates were outraged by my conclusions and, perhaps revealingly, even that I had studied the subject at all. But numerous current and former U.S. (and foreign) intelligence officers advocated the follow-on study. Many of them offered anecdotes strongly suggesting that DEI policies in fact damage agencies' operational performance. Many of those anecdotes and insights, and others from other sources, appear in this book.

Neither position has yet been well supported in published studies beyond small snippets of evidence and logic, however. But unlike the ethical argument, performance claims are at least potentially testable. A note on methodology therefore is important. This study identified and examined evidence related to the operational effects of DEI policies—positive and negative. The data include public sources as well as the

---

[16] Roger Hesketh, *Fortitude: The D-Day Deception Campaign* (Woodstock NY: Overlook, 2000).

[17] John A. Gentry, "Demographic Diversity in U.S. Intelligence Personnel: Is It Functionally Useful?" *International Journal of Intelligence and CounterIntelligence* 36:2 (2023): 564-596. For the requirement that analyses be fact-based, see the third iteration of Intelligence Community Directive 203, "Analytic Standards," December 21, 2022, page 3.

author's extensive contacts with current and former intelligence officers, many of whom provided information on confidential bases. Tellingly, many sources wish to remain anonymous because they believe they would be harmed if it were known that they provided such information to this study, whose very existence is politically incorrect in some quarters. Hence, many personal sources are unnamed but described only generically. All sources cited, including the anonymous ones, have first-hand knowledge of information reported herein.

The cited sources tell stories very similar to those of 23 then-serving Federal Bureau of Investigation (FBI) employees who reported on DEI-related problems at their agency in 2023.[18] This book focuses on foreign-oriented U.S. intelligence services, but DEI policies of successive presidents have pertained to the entire federal workforce. Hence, the experiences of FBI personnel in related law enforcement and counterintelligence work are relevant to, and nicely complement, this study.

The findings of this study are important because, if critics of DEI policies are right, DEI has potentially significant and strategically negative ramifications for the national security of states that adopt such policies. It really is true that intelligence is the first line of national defense. Policymakers therefore need to know which perspective is more accurate. The security of Western states individually and collectively is at stake. DEI-like perspectives also have infiltrated other Western countries and their intelligence services, sparking controversy in several countries, prominently including Canada.[19] This study is the first to attempt to assess the performance question's causal mechanisms with any degree of rigor. It addresses the veracity of various claims that DEI policies harm or help foreign-focused intelligence services, leaving aside the somewhat different but also very serious issue of DEI's effects on U.S. military

---

[18] National Alliance of Retired and Active-Duty FBI Special Agents and Analysts, "Report on Alarming Trends in FBI Special Agent Recruitment and Selection," October 2023, 37-52, 67-69, 80-96, https://www.scribd.com/document/701275030/Report-on-FBI-Special-Agent-Recruitment-and-Selection. This report hereafter is cited as "National Alliance, 'Report.'"
[19] See, for example, the summer 2023 edition (volume 23, number 3) of the *Canadian Military Journal*, www.journal.forces.gc.ca/cmj-23.3-toc-en.html.

organizations.[20] It especially assesses the Central Intelligence Agency (CIA).

In sum, this study finds appreciable evidence that DEI policies significantly damage the operational performance of U.S. intelligence and no evidence that DEI improves its performance. This effectively debunks the ideological nature of claims by Clapper, Medina, and others, and offers an explanation of why my work has been denied publication elsewhere and why some hold even my addressing the subject to be controversial. As has been the case in other national institutions (e.g. corporations, schools, universities, media organizations), DEI policies have systematically changed core cultural norms and processes in ways that damage intelligence practices. This threatens to weaken the agencies' support of national decisionmakers and thus endangers U.S. national security. The full magnitude of DEI-induced dysfunctions and their consequences may not yet be known, however, because our adversaries have not yet exploited national security vulnerabilities caused by DEI-related intelligence failures and weaknesses. The inherent secrecy surrounding intelligence also limits the volume and completeness of publicly available information about the quality and uses of intelligence. U.S. intelligence agencies rarely study themselves via large-scale surveys, generally do not divulge them publicly, and never permit outsiders to do so.[21] Unlike other organizations that have studied the effects of DEI policies and sometimes rejected them as harmful, the agencies have refused to study the issue of DEI's effect on operational performance in any way, instead relying on assumptions and ideological assertions that are daunting, and possibly dangerous, to challenge. This study offers a thorough analytic approach supported by evidence to stimulate additional research and theorizing. A more detailed,

---

[20] Matthew Lohmeier, *Irresistible Revolution: Marxism's Goal of Conquest & the Unmaking of the American Military* (self-published, 2021). See also, Arizona State University, Center for American Institutions, *Civic Education in the Military*, n.d., https://cai.asu.edu/sites/default/files/2024-06/CAI%20Civic%20Education%20in%20the%20Military%20Report%20-%20Digital%20v3.pdf.

[21] This author is aware of only one large-scale such study in the public domain, conducted by cultural anthropologist and CIA employee Rob Johnston, *Analytic Culture in the U.S. Intelligence Community: An Ethnographic Study* (Washington: Central Intelligence Agency, Center for the Study of Intelligence, 2005).

data-rich examination, however, may await the work of a commission investigating the causes of the next big intelligence failure.

Chapter 2

The Intellectual and Policy Background

The DEI perspective, as we now know it, is a relatively recent phenomenon. Its intellectual history is easily traced to Marxist "critical" theories produced by scholars of the *Institut für Sozialforschung* (Institute for Social Research) at the Goethe University in Frankfurt, Germany, an intellectual community commonly known as the "Frankfurt School," which dates to 1923.[1] During the Nazi era, most members of the Frankfurt School relocated to the United States, where they began instructing generations of American intellectuals in their philosophy, which included the idea that a Marxist transformation of society could be effected on a cultural level, through institutions of civic life.

All Marxist "critical" theories use similar terminology, cite similar historical antecedents, and were developed by people who have overtly expressed their commitments to Marxism. Other Marxists often hide their true intellectual loyalties in order to avoid offending nonbelievers, ensuring some faux outrage at this observation of fact. "Critical theory" has many spin-offs, including "critical legal studies" that attempt to use the law to advance political goals, "critical pedagogy" that instructs teachers how to indoctrinate their students in Marxist categories of thought and judgment, and "critical race theory," which views all social, economic, and political relations through a lens of racist oppression. DEI is a direct intellectual descendant of critical race theory.

Critical theory's most recent incarnation, and popular use of the acronym DEI, is a creation of President Barack Obama, who promised to

---

[1] Rolf Wiggershaus, *The Frankfurt School: Its History, Theories, and Political Significance* (Cambridge MA: MIT Press, 1995).

"transform" America just before he was elected in 2008.[2] He spoke extensively about the importance of preferential treatment for politically favored domestic demographic "identity" groups, especially blacks, women, and LGBTQ+ people—member groups of what is often called the "Obama Coalition" of supporters of the Democratic Party. Obama made demographic diversity one of his major priorities.[3] DEI thus became a core component of what Obama and his supporters frequently called "our values."[4]

Obama and his followers appear to have ignored federal laws that ban discrimination in employment. The major federal law regarding workplace discrimination is the Civil Rights Act of 1964, which prohibits discriminatory employment decisions or actions based on a person's race, color, religion, sex, national origin, and other "protected characteristics," including, via a recent Supreme Court decision, sexual orientation (42 U.S.C. § 2000e-2).[5] The U.S. Equal Employment Opportunity Commission is charged with enforcing workplace discrimination laws, including the Civil Rights Act of 1964, or authorizing their enforcement through the legal system.

While some of the major DEI policy documents published by IC agencies give passing nods to the old virtues of functional diversity—of outlooks, foreign experiences, language expertise, and other skills related to the practice of intelligence by individuals—the new emphasis, following Obama, is demographic, group-oriented, and political in motivation. That is, it refers to characteristics of Americans, not the foreigners whom the foreign-focused intelligence agencies study. Contrary to some academic advocates of DEI who argue that racially diverse campuses offer greater intellectual advantages—despite the fact

---

[2] David Weigel, "'Fundamentally Transforming the United States of America,'" *Slate*, October 18, 2011, https://slate.com/news-and-politics/2011/10/fundamentally-transforming-the-united-states-of-america.html.

[3] The Obama White House, "Strengthening Civil Rights," n.d., https://obamawhite house.archives.gov/issues/civil-rights/empowerment.

[4] For example, President Barack Obama comments, May 21, 2009, https://obamawhite house.archives.gov/video/President-Obama-Our-Security-Our-Values#transcript.

[5] Nelson Lim, Abigail Haddad, and Lindsay Daugherty, *Implementation of the DoD Diversity and Inclusion Strategic Plan: A Framework for Change Through Accountability* (Santa Monica CA: RAND, 2013), 17.

that many demographic groups are expected to display political views consistent with stereotypical perspectives of their group identity—or that "lived experiences" define relative truth, Yale University Professor Anthony Kronman has argued, and some polling data confirm, that diversity enhancement efforts on university campuses have led to expectations that specified identify groups should think and act in stereotypical ways, resulting in a sharp drop in the intellectual diversity that is ostensibly at the heart of university life.[6] Kronman's argument seems especially applicable to young IC employees who are recent products of ideological indoctrination programs now common on college campuses. The federal government makes no such direct claims. Instead, as the ODNI recounts on its website, its efforts and its annual reports of the IC's demography, now required by law, recount the "IC's struggle to recruit talented officers who mirror the diverse country they serve."[7] The mirror metaphor is apt because the explicit goal of DEI is to make the federal workforce, and the IC, visually "look like America." In a notable irony, however, in June 2023 the Supreme Court ruled that the use of race in college admissions decisions is unlawful.

It is important to emphasize that this view strenuously opposes the IC's traditional concept of desirable diversity—intellectual diversity within individuals that reflects understanding NOT of the population of the United States, but of the world outside of the United States, where the mainly foreign-focused IC agencies operate and which they try to comprehend. By traditional reasoning, intellectual diversity helps intelligence organizations collectively think broadly and deeply, and thereby perform better. Pioneering CIA analyst Sherman Kent argued as long ago as 1949 that any good intelligence service should have room for the "queer bird and eccentric with a unique talent" even if he is occasionally wrong—a concept foreign to DEI thinking, which insists that its tenets are always correct, or at least unfalsifiable.[8]

---

[6] Anthony Kronman, "The Downside of Diversity," *Wall Street Journal*, 3-4 August 2019, C1.

[7] ODNI, "Diversity & Inclusion," n.d., https://www.dni.gov/ind, 2013).ex.php/how-we-work/diversity.

[8] Sherman Kent, *Strategic Intelligence for American World Policy* (Princeton: Princeton University Press, 1949), 74.

U.S. intelligence has long recognized its need for some racial diversity in order to operate in a big world that "looks" substantially different than the population of the United States. When operating in Sri Lanka, for example, it makes sense for U.S. intelligence officers to "look like," and act like, they hail from Colombo, not Cleveland. To emphasize another important point, it has long been clear to U.S. intelligence agencies, and to reputable external observers, that persons from all significant demographic groups can be, and are, capable intelligence officers. In all cases, they are capable (or not) as individuals, not because of their membership in a large demographic identity group.[9]

The old IC concept of trying to find and deploy diversity of outlook, education, and experience in individuals as tools of effective performance has therefore been deemphasized, if not yet entirely gone. Evidence of this change now is abundant. Officials say so regularly, but usually implicitly, by emphasizing DEI as a variety of identity politics. Annual reports on the demographic diversity of the intelligence workforce contain no performance metrics or even any discussion of the desirability of developing such measures. Questioning the efficacy of any aspect of DEI policies, or suggesting that claims about the performance implications of DEI policies should be tested, have been, and remain, politically incorrect. Doing so is bureaucratically dangerous for federal employees and for scholars who study DEI issues at similarly "woke" universities and in other institutions. Illiberal intolerance of such questioning is a serious and still growing threat to many people.[10]

---

[9] Gentry, "Demographic Diversity in U.S. Intelligence Personnel."

[10] This illiberal intolerance closely resembles that advocated by Herbert Marcuse, a Frankfurt School activist. See his "Repressive Tolerance," in Robert Paul Wolff, Barrington Moore Jr., and Herbert Marcuse, *A Critique of Pure Tolerance* (Boston: Beacon, 1969), 81-123.

Chapter 3

DEI in the Intelligence Community

The issue of whether, and how, DEI policies affect the operational performance of the IC has remained unexplored despite a growing number of relevant anecdotes and improved understanding of how DEI-reengineered processes can cause intelligence dysfunction. Assessing the merits of this controversy is not easy. Government performance in general is notoriously hard to assess. Most government agencies perform public services without payment by "customers," whose reactions in other contexts measure quality using such traditional business metrics as sales, profits, ratings, or return on investment. Given the inherent secrecy of most intelligence activities, evidence documenting their performance is limited. No one has yet developed persuasive methods of assessing the performance of intelligence agencies in aggregate, although a few aspects of performance potentially can be measured.[1] Hence, a major challenge is the creation of an analytic method or model that can credibly assess the DEI controversy. No U.S. presidential administration has investigated the issue or purposefully released data relevant to this research question. What follows is a first attempt to meet this challenge.

To argue convincingly that DEI policies effect performance, the first task is to specify a chain of causally linked events from policymaking through bureaucratic processes to outcomes that can be assessed, at least qualitatively. U.S. intelligence agencies vary in function and structure but most, and the CIA by law, focus on activities in foreign countries. The agencies collect information and turn it into intelligence through analysis. This process is well known in the intelligence studies literature; one

---

[1] John A. Gentry, "Assessing Intelligence Performance," in Loch K. Johnson, ed., *Oxford Handbook of National Security Intelligence*, 2nd ed.,. (Oxford University Press, forthcoming).

prominent such model is the "intelligence cycle."[2] The agencies also conduct a variety of operations abroad, in recent years in Iraq and Afghanistan in paramilitary-related missions such as counterterrorism. The CIA does all of these things, as well as presidentially directed covert actions, for which we have considerable data about organizational structures and cultures, bureaucratic processes, operational practices, and operational results. My analytical approach thus applies primarily to the CIA but will have obvious implications for other agencies that have incorporated DEI policies into their missions.

First in the causal chain are DEI-related presidential policies, including executive orders (EOs), other formal and sometimes legally binding requirements, and verbal directives. Surely there is plenty of less formal guidance, but public records of it are scarce. Individual accounts typically are subjective, brief, and anecdotal, and may be self-serving. EOs in principle are binding on federal employees, although compliance appears to be spotty, driven by the political attitudes of the bureaucrats who receive them. Despite the CIA's ostensible subordination to the Director of National Intelligence (DNI) per the Intelligence Reform and Terrorism Prevention Act of 2004 (IRTPA), the agency still generally works directly for the President without departmental secretaries or the DNI as intermediaries.

Second, the Director of National Intelligence, the senior U.S. intelligence officer, and diversity offices employing delegated authority, issue policy guidance, informally or via formal orders including "intelligence community directives," or ICDs, applicable to the IC as a whole. Some ICDs are personal orders; others are products of collective decision making by IC agencies that the DNI simply signs.[3] DNIs communicate their views in a variety of other ways, including speeches and organized forums, for example. Unlike presidents, DNIs do not have executive powers over IC organizations other than the ODNI. They share power over other agencies with the President in the case of the CIA and

---

[2] For example, Arthur S. Hulnick, "What's wrong with the Intelligence Cycle," *Intelligence and National Security* 21:6 (2006): 959-979.

[3] John A. Gentry, "Has the ODNI Improved U.S. Intelligence Analysis?" *International Journal of Intelligence and CounterIntelligence* 28:4 (2015): 637-661.

with the department secretaries for other agencies. Hence, agencies sometimes regard compliance with DNI policies as optional.

Third, agency heads, including the Director of the CIA (DCIA), convert presidential and ODNI policies and other guidances into their own policies that fit their specific missions, organizations, and, in many cases, their personal preferences, but normally in ways roughly consistent with more senior-level guidance. This is done via strategy documents, policy directives, and managerial decisions. The heads of the CIA's five directorates convert them into policies tailored to their distinctive organizational structures, missions, and daily practices. In some cases, senior executives have admitted that they intended to change the organizational cultures of their agencies or sub-units in politically relevant ways—a complicated, time-consuming process—often citing DEI as a policy goal or a tool of process.

Fourth, the policies influence human resources administration, including decisions in hiring, promotions, assignments, and awards. They also affect the nature and terms of the resolution of employees' complaints against management and other employees. During the Obama administration, these policies shifted from standing "equal employment opportunity" and "affirmative action" policies to explicit preferences for privileged demographic identity groups defined by DEI doctrine. Over time, the policies and practices appreciably changed the demography and collective politics of the IC.[4] Beyond the scope of discussion here, these policies have also applied to federal contractors, changing the extended IC workforce similarly.

Fifth, DEI policies are implemented using resources allocated by formal budget processes, including those of the White House, the Office of Management and Budget, Congress, the IC as a whole as represented by the ODNI, and individual agencies such as the CIA. Some funds are devoted specifically to DEI-motivated purposes, while others support DEI-related aspects of usual operational activities. Managers then deploy their people and existing physical resources in ways consistent with DEI priorities.

---

[4] John A. Gentry, *Neutering the CIA: Why US Intelligence Versus Trump Has Long-Term Consequences* (Estes Park CO: Armin Lear, 2023), 134-139.

Sixth, diversity offices at each agency make DEI-related policies using powers delegated to them by agency heads and operationalize them by implementing actions, such as requiring employees to complete DEI-focused training. At the CIA, these actions are further refined by directorate-level diversity offices and newer diversity offices at the next level down in each directorate. In the Directorate of Operations (DO), these are called divisions; in the Directorate of Analysis (DA), they are offices. Both types of units are organized along regional or functional lines. In addition, as a result of a major CIA reorganization in 2015, regionally and functionally focused "mission centers" are matrixed organizations composed of both DO and DA personnel. Mission centers also have diversity offices. Employees can file complaints with diversity officers if they believe they have not been managed in accordance with agency DEI policies—or their own wishes if framed in DEI jargon. Diversity offices thus often become the "go-to" offices for disgruntled employees, competing with or replacing the inspectors general who previously handled some serious personnel grievances.

Seventh, line managers implement policies encouraged or enforced by their own incentive structures through day-to-day operational decisions as well as in promotion, assignment, and award decisions. Usually, these are the immediate drivers of operational consequences of DEI-related policies. Managers also address some diversity-related complaints.

Eighth, policies are acted upon—as in the processes of analysis or human intelligence collection, the CIA's two major operational performance arenas. Scholars of intelligence have only an incomplete understanding of ways in which DEI-related decisions influence actual operations. Independent of DEI concerns, leaders' decisions have operational implications in areas such as shaping the contents of published analytic papers, agents recruited or not, priority information needs collected or not, paramilitary or counterterrorist operational successes or failures, and so on. DEI affects these processes in different ways. Some relevant data are public information. These include formal DEI-focused publications, such as demographic data, as well as a growing number of leaked reports of DEI-related dysfunctions. Agency reactions to these leaks vary. By many accounts, the FBI has strenuously attacked DEI-related leakers and "whistleblowers."[5] In contrast, the CIA appears to remain, as of this writing, relatively unconcerned about leaks of politically sensitive information that do not include classified material. These reports have affected perceptions of the agencies by senior decision makers, fellow bureaucrats, lawmakers, commentators, and ordinary citizens, making them "operational results" of a different sort. Increasingly, DEI-influenced policies are disparaged, and therefore not taken seriously, meaning the work and resources poured into them has been wasted, possibly at the cost of effective intelligence operations.

Ideally, we should be able to track DEI-related policies from policy origination to operational outcome in ways that reveal causality. This offers analysis much like the "process tracing" technique employed in the social sciences.[6] Nevertheless, the detailed understanding of intelligence needed for such tracing is rarely possible due to secrecy restrictions and the sheer complexity of the operations of large organizations that interact with other agencies of their own government as well as (often) many other actors in complicated operational environments.[7] Limited data availability and undefined quality standards make it impossible for outsiders to conduct academic-style longitudinal studies with the independent and dependent variables that social scientists employ. For these reasons, the extant intelligence studies literature contains no large-scale statistical studies of any aspect of national intelligence.

My effort takes a "next-best" approach, arguing, on the basis of a fairly detailed understanding of the structures and basic processes that CIA elements employ, that activities and decisions at each stage of the

---

[5] For example, Committee on the Judiciary and the Select Subcommittee on the Weaponization of the Federal Government, "FBI WHISTLEBLOWER TESTIMONY HIGHLIGHTS GOVERNMENT ABUSE, MISALLOCATION OF RESOURCES, AND RETALIATION," May 18, 2023, https://judiciary.house.gov/sites/evo-subsites/republicans-judiciary.house.gov/files/evo-media-document/2023-05-17-fbi-whistleblower-testimony-highlights-government-abuse-misallocation-of-resources-and-retaliation-sm.pdf.

[6] Derek Beach, "Process Tracing Methods in the Social Sciences," Oxford Research Encyclopedias, January 25, 2017, https://oxfordre.com/politics/display/10.1093/acrefore/9780190228637.001.0001/acrefore-9780190228637-e-176.

[7] Robert W. Komer, *Bureaucracy at War: U.S. Performance in the Vietnam Conflict* (Abingdon, UK: Routledge, 2021).

intelligence process both reflect higher-level policies and influence lower-level policies and activities. In this way, this study explains much of how and why DEI policies and DEI-related actions interact at each stage and ultimately influence operational outcomes without knowing the details of all operations. The National Alliance's "Report" takes a similar though less explicit approach, examining causes (such as organizational ideology, recruiting standards, and training) before discussing operational problems evidently caused by the FBI's DEI policies.[8] That large numbers of tangentially related vignettes all point in the same direction should give readers confidence about the accuracy of the general patterns described herein.

---

[8] National Alliance, "Report."

Chapter 4

DEI Policies in Action

DEI policies move through many stages before they affect intelligence activities and national security. This chapter outlines these stages in detail and links them procedurally. While clearly similar in some respects, these activities differ appreciably from DEI-related effects in businesses, universities, and the military.

Presidential directives

The U.S. government, and therefore the intelligence agencies, long have embraced "affirmative action," a bipartisan 1960s-era presidential initiative to give modest preferences to racial minorities and women in federal hiring decisions. The motive was political, not functional. The CIA's leaders long ago also recognized that, given the global responsibilities presidents gave them after the agency's founding in 1947, it needed to recruit a wide variety of talent relevant to global missions, wherever and in whomever they could be found. Hence, CIA and other agencies sought to find skills that would help them perform their relatively narrow legally and administratively defined functions—especially the collection and analysis of *foreign* information relevant to American national decision making. Domestically defined "lived experiences" and other currently fashionable notions irrelevant to these missions were not acquired. The CIA thereby gradually expanded its sources of relevant human expertise—regionally, racially, and by hiring more women—but not fast enough for critics.[1]

---

[1] For example, Brent Durbin, "Addressing 'This Woeful Imbalance': Efforts to Improve Women's Representation at CIA, 1947–2014," *Intelligence and National Security* 30:6 (2015): 855-870.

Previous discrimination against women and minorities led to a bipartisan desire to give individuals from these groups modest advantages in hiring and promotions via affirmative action. President Bill Clinton (1993-2001) accelerated this effort somewhat, and President George W. Bush (2001-2009) maintained it. But while they emphasized hiring women and minorities, in the early years affirmative action policies did not state, or even suggest, that the preferences should trump merit or ability. "Equal employment opportunity" remained government policy. While there were some accusations that persons hired under affirmative action programs were underqualified, they seem to have been few in number and often, but not always, unfounded. All of this changed dramatically in 2009.

President Barack Obama

President Barack Obama (2009-2017) went far further on "affirmative action" than any of his predecessors. On October 30, 2008, just before he won the presidential election, he said at a rally, "We are five days away from fundamentally transforming the United States of America."[2] Obama's key transformative policy document relative to the federal workforce was Executive Order (EO) 13583 of August 18, 2011, "Establishing a Coordinated Government-Wide Initiative to Promote Diversity and Inclusion in the Federal Workforce." This order summarized his explicitly political, widely touted agenda, which soon became known popularly as the government version of DEI.[3] Other variants quickly developed in universities and businesses. This program differed markedly from the language of the Intelligence Reform and Terrorism Prevention Act of 2004, which required the IC to prescribe personnel policies and programs ensuring that its personnel "are sufficiently diverse for purposes of the collection and analysis of intelligence through the recruitment and training of women, minorities, and individuals with diverse ethnic, cultural, and linguistic backgrounds"—a performance-motivated

---

[2] David Weigel, "'Fundamentally Changing the United States of America,'" *Slate*, October 11, 2011, https://slate.com/news-and-politics/2011/10/fundamentally-transforming-the-united-states-of-america.html.
[3] Available at https://obamawhitehouse.archives.gov/the-press-office/2011/08/18/executive-order-13583-establishing-coordinated-government-wide-initiativ.
Businesses and universities conduct DEI programs differently.

objective consistent with previous IC policies.[4] Obama made old varieties of affirmative action passé. Indeed, the term itself is no longer widely used and has been broadly superseded by DEI.

Obama and his appointees said explicitly, and repeatedly, that the goal of his DEI program was to hire and promote more people from favored demographic groups—a strong variety of preferential identity politics. Federal employees as a whole should "look like America," said Obama, his appointees, and many of the people his policies advantaged. Members of Obama's favored identity groups thereby became privileged in the sense that they enjoyed, and still enjoy, a large number of administrative and professional advantages as matters of formal, clearly stated policy and, in some cases, law. It soon became clear that changes in the demographic composition and, thereby, the political complexion of the federal workforce were major Obama priorities. This political commitment, and the tangible material benefits provided to privileged demographic groups, largely explain many individuals' strong commitment to DEI. Former CIA director John Brennan, who was a close White House aide to Obama in 2009-2013, wrote that Obama was "an advocate of evolutionary change rather than violent upheaval."[5] DEI became a useful tool of slow and as yet non-violent revolutionary change.

The U.S. Government Accountability Office (GAO) has two "benchmarks" that many parts of the government, including the IC, often use for comparative purposes in the context of DEI: groups' share of the federal workforce and of the civilian workforce.[6] These measures were not always helpful to support Obama's diversity agenda in the IC, however, leading to a shifting set of comparisons over time by various IC leaders, who use(d) different standards (such as numbers for groups at higher pay

---

[4] Congressional Research Service, "Intelligence Community Diversity and Equal Opportunity," R44269, summary, October 2020, file:///C:/Users/Owner/Documents/Publications-of-Interest/CRS-IC-Diversity-Equal-Opportunity-Strategy.pdf.

[5] John O. Brennan, *Undaunted: My Fight Against America's Enemies at Home and Abroad* (New York: Celadon, 2020), 251.

[6] U.S. Government Accountability Office, *Intelligence Community: Additional Actions Needed to Strengthen Workforce Diversity Planning and Oversight*, GAO-21-83, December 2020, 3. ODNI, "Annual Demographic Report Fiscal Year 2020," July 8, 2021, https:// www.odni.gov/files/EEOD/documents/IC_Annual_Demographic_Report.pdf, 10.

grades and shares of promotions to each grade) to justify continuing hiring and promotion preferences for privileged demographic groups.[7] The government employment benchmarks were and remain very useful for rationalizing the hiring of people of sub-Saharan African descent, however. At the end of Obama's second term, in 2016, blacks were roughly proportionately represented in the IC in relation to their share of the U.S. population but were overrepresented in the federal workforce as a whole by about 42 percent.[8] Blacks generally hold lower-ranking, lower paid positions, however. Because the black share of the U.S. government workforce is far above blacks' share of the population and of the civilian workforce, one can conclude that DEI-inspired race-based preferences elaborated in relevant policy documents account for part of the excess.

President Donald Trump

President Trump (2017-2021) did surprisingly little to alter Obama's DEI policies, especially given their role in generating partisan political activism in opposition to him beginning in 2016, discussed below. Trump said negative things about some of his intelligence critics, especially former CIA director John Brennan, and made periodic threats that he generally did not follow through with.[9] For example, he pledged in his 2016 campaign to "drain the swamp" of bureaucrats in Washington but did essentially nothing in this arena when he was in office.

Trump made no direct DEI-related moves until September 22, 2020 – nearly the end of his presidency – when he abolished mandatory "unconscious bias" training for federal workers and federal contractors – a small part of the large complex of DEI-related policies and programs then in effect.[10] Apparently, he and his team did not believe that DEI was

---

[7] Gentry, *Neutering the CIA*, 165, 168.

[8] Office of the Director of National Intelligence, "Annual Demographic Report: Hiring and Retention of Minorities, Women, and Persons with Disabilities in the United States Intelligence Community Fiscal Year 2016," 46.

[9] For example, Max Greenwood, "Trump calls Brennan a 'very bad person' after Putin criticism," *The Hill*, July 17, 2018, http://thehill.com/homenews/administration/397 437-trump-calls-brennan-a-very-bad-person-after-putin-criticism.

[10] NPR staff, "Trump Expands Ban On Racial Sensitivity Training to Federal Contractors, NPR, September 22, 2020, https://www.npr.org/2020/09/22/9158434 71/trump-expands-ban-on-racial-sensitivity-training-to-federal-contractors.

a problem earlier, and indeed, discussion of it at that time was confined to a small number of conservative activists who ironically rose in prominence after Trump left office. This order immediately was challenged in court and had minimal effect given that it happened so near the end of his term.[11] Joe Biden rescinded it promptly upon entering office in January 2021. With Obama-era preferences for women remaining operative throughout the Trump years, by 2020 the CIA's staff was almost equally male and female, substantially exceeding both of the GAO's benchmarks (women then were 43.2% of the federal workforce and 47.0% of the civilian economy-wide workforce).[12]

President Joe Biden

President Biden (2021-2025) pledged to have the most demographically diverse administration in American history, and by many accounts did so. He often crowed about his achievement. He reenergized and expanded Obama-era personnel policies throughout the federal government by issuing a series of aggressive executive orders along with substantial command emphasis that pushed an expanded diversity agenda.[13] On Biden's first day in office, he signed EO 13985, "Advancing Racial Equity and Support for Underserved Communities Throughout the Federal Government."[14] This title is a misnomer; historic U.S. government and Biden policies *abundantly* serve privileged identity groups. More importantly, Biden issued EO 14035, "Advancing Diversity, Equity, Inclusion, and Accessibility (DEIA) in the Federal Workforce," in June

---

[11] Melissa Block, "Agencies, Contractors Suspend Diversity Training To Avoid Violating Trump Order," NPR, October 30, 2020, https://www.npr.org/2020/10/30/929165869/agencies-contractors-suspend-diversity-training-to-avoid-violating-trump-order.

[12] ODNI, "Annual Demographic Report Fiscal Year 2020," 10.

[13] For example, The White House, "Executive Order on Diversity, Equity, Inclusion, and Accessibility in the Federal Workforce, June 25, 2021, https://www.whitehouse.gov/briefing-room/presidential-actions/2021/06/25/executive-order-on-diversity-equity-inclusion-and-accessibility-in-the-federal-workforce/.

[14] EO at https://www.federalregister.gov/documents/2021/01/25/2021-01753/advancing-racial-equity-and-support-for-underserved-communities-through-the-federal-government.

2021.[15] This order substantially increased preferences for disabled persons. Hence the "A," for "Accessibility," in the new formulation DEIA.

Like Obama's EO 13585, Biden's order has sharp enforcement teeth. Biden's Office of Personnel Management (OPM), for example, soon issued guidance on how it intended to ensure that EO 14035 would be implemented, including timelines for implementation.[16] First, agencies were to submit self-assessments of their current state of DEIA compliance to OPM. Then the government's detailed strategic plan would be issued, followed by agencies' strategic plans and then, on a continuing annual basis, agencies' compliance "progress reports." The Office of Management and Budget (OMB) and the Equal Employment Opportunity Commission (EEOC), along with OPM, were to monitor progress and enforce the policies.

Initially, Obama and his appointees championed DEI policies as ethically good—they purportedly helped redress discrimination in previous eras—a political line the Biden administration also follows. DEI is consistent with "our values," it was frequently said. But it soon became clear that partisan political and ideological motives, not merely ethical standards of fairness, were at work in ways consistent with the fact that DEI policies at heart spring from identity politics, which themselves reflect Marxist notions about the desirability of dividing people into groups with collective identity traits that can be characterized as being in antagonistic, dyadic oppressor-oppressed relationships. The old "equal opportunity employment" mantra faded in the Obama years and became virtually non-existent in the Biden years. The longstanding American tradition of treating people as individuals, each with his or her own characteristics, was marginalized.

DEI policies thus transparently were not only about providing material advantages for favored demographic groups—as groups, not as individuals—they were about empowering newly privileged groups

---

[15] White House Fact Sheet, https://www.whitehouse.gov/briefing-room/presidential-actions/2021/06/25/executive-order-on-diversity-equity-inclusion-and-accessibility-in-the-federal-workforce/.

[16] OPM website, n.d., https://www.opm.gov/policy-data-oversight/diversity-equity-inclusion-and-accessibility/reference-materials/diversity-equity-inclusion-accessibility-in-the-federal-workforce.pdf.

politically. In the Obama years, this goal appeared tangibly in newly created "affinity groups"—which also are known as "employee resource groups"—at federal agencies. The role of these groups is to promote solidarity among their members and resist supposed "oppression" by white males within their agencies. In the Biden years, these groups were reemphasized, especially in their relation to "whiteness" and masculinity, which are increasingly described as "toxic." Many of Obama's and Biden's supporters have not been shy about making such claims as key parts of their DEI agenda, though their assertions usually are softened though use of obfuscating terminology or language that means different things to Marxists, on the one hand, and most American citizens, on the other.[17] For example, DEI advocates claim that their policies will help achieve "social justice"—a surely uncontroversial goal on its face but one with vastly different definitions in the current climate.

Government agencies' "affinity groups" of people of similar demographic identities have also helped ensure ideological orthodoxy of these "oppressed" groups. The groups were not intended to be merely social clubs, but "safe" places where employees are encouraged complain about their white, male, and heterosexual "oppressors." Some meetings reportedly resemble "struggle sessions" devoted to enforcing ideological conformity that foreign communist parties often require of their members. They also helped trigger the outburst of partisan political activism against Trump in 2016—and may again in future election years—a dramatic change from longstanding IC norms and a good measure of the substantial success Obama, Clapper, Brennan, and others had in changing them.

Intellectual history

While the intellectual origins of DEI spring from the Frankfurt School of German Marxists, who developed "critical theories" that were designed to identify, or help create, cultural divisions that Marxist ideology could exploit, theories and practices directly relevant to DEI are more recent. A

---

[17] John A. Gentry, "Ideology in Costume: A Growing Threat to Intelligence Studies," *International Journal of Intelligence and CounterIntelligence* 37:2 (2024): 751-774; Gary Saul Morson, "Marxism Is a Gulag of the Mind," *Wall Street Journal*, May 15, 2024, A17.

large literature documents this intellectual history, much of which is not directly germane to a discussion of DEI policies or their effects.

"Critical legal studies" emerged in the 1970s and 1980s in the thought of a small community of American and British law school professors, such as Derrick Bell and Kimberlé Crenshaw, who argued that social conditions they disliked—especially the alleged oppression of black people—were inextricably linked to prevailing legal structures.[18] They argued that the law should be used as a tool of praxis to facilitate achievement of their political objectives.

"Critical race theory," today best exemplified by the work of Ibram X. Kendi (born Henry Rogers) and Robin DiAngelo, holds that all whites – including children and babies – are inherently racist and asserts that society must change to bring "equity" in all measurable ways to black people.[19] This is the origin of the "E," for "Equity," in DEI, which sounds vaguely like "Equality," a foundational American concept to which hardly anyone would object. It is, CRT advocates opine, not merely appropriate but necessary to discriminate against whites in order to achieve the desired "equity." "The only remedy to racist discrimination is antiracist discrimination," wrote Kendi, adding that "the only remedy to past discrimination is present discrimination," while "the only remedy to present discrimination is future discrimination."[20] Crenshaw asserted that heterosexual men of European origin "oppress" all other people and urged "intersectional" groups, or persons from multiple demographic categories, like black women such as herself, to fight such "oppression" together.[21] Hence the division of the federal workforce into demographically defined "affinity groups" that "ally" with each other to pursue DEI-oriented goals.

To ensure that such ideas spread, Marxists in the 1980s developed "critical pedagogy," or a doctrine of how to instruct teachers to

---

[18] Derrick A. Bell, *Race, Racism, and American Law*, 6th ed. (Los Angeles CA: Aspen Publishers, 2008).

[19] For example, Ibram X. Kendi, *How to Be an Antiracist* (New York: One World, 2019); Robin DiAngelo, *White Fragility: Why It's So Hard for White People to Talk About Racism* (Boston: Beacon, 2018).

[20] Kendi, *How to Be an Antiracist*, 19.

[21] Kimberlé Crenshaw, "Mapping the Margins: Intersectionality, Identity Politics, and Violence Against Women of Color," *Stanford Law Review* 43:6 (1991): 1241-1299.

indoctrinate their students with Marxist ideas, an approach that now dominates schools of education at American universities.[22] Critical pedagogy reflects the pioneering work of Brazilian Marxist Paulo Freire, who aimed to develop a doctrine of how to "educate" people by playing to their grievances and aspirations in order to instill Marxist perspectives.[23] The overtly stated primary goal of this "education" is political indoctrination of students, not traditional reading, writing, and arithmetic, which Freire derided as "banking" education that is allegedly an instrument of oppression.[24] Cultural Marxists such as Antonio Gramsci long ago noted the importance of ideological indoctrination under the guise of education, and his followers advocated a "march through the institutions" to ensure conformity of thought.[25] Implementing techniques now include the use of drag queens, who offer "story hours" to confuse young children about sexual realities, part of the long-running Marxist effort to destroy nuclear families.

This indoctrination, now widespread at American universities but encountering significant pushback, helped prepare younger IC employees to respond positively to DEI-related initiatives in the Obama years and beyond. Government DEI training programs appear to feature content consistent with principles of critical pedagogy, a development that has been noted in studies of the military service academies[26] and even in the K-12 education taught at Defense Department of Defense-run schools[27] for the children of military personnel and of some Defense Department civilian employees.

---

[22] For example, Antonia Darder et al., ed., *The Critical Pedagogy Reader*, 3rd ed. (Milton Park, UK: Routledge, 2017).
[23] Freire's two most prominent works, translated into English, are *Pedagogy of the Oppressed* (New York: Penguin, 2017), originally published in 1968, and *The Politics of Education: Culture, Power, and Liberation* (Hadley MA: Bergin & Garvey, 1985).
[24] Freire, *Pedagogy of the Oppressed*, 7.
[25] Antonio Gramsci, *Selections from the Prison Notebooks* (New York: International Publishers, 1971), 24-43.
[26] Arizona State University, Center for American Institutions, *Civic Education in the Military*, n.d., https://cai.asu.edu/sites/default/files/2024-06/CAI%20Civic%20Education%20in%20the%20Military%20Report%20-%20Digital%20v3.pdf.
[27] Openthebooks.com, "Pentagon's Secret Push to Institutionalize DEI in Its K-12 Public Schools," July 2024, https://www.openthebooks.com/assets/1/6/Culture_of_Secrecy_at_DoDEA2.pdf?utm_source=substack&utm_medium=email.

Obama was well aware of these intellectual trends. By many accounts, he was mentored influentially as a teenager and young man by Frank Marshall Davis, a black member of the Communist Party of the USA.[28] Better known is that while Obama was a "community organizer" in Chicago before entering electoral politics, he befriended Bill Ayers and Bernadine Dohrn, founders of the Weather Underground group of radical terrorists of the late 1960s and early 1970s. He also interacted with the controversial Reverend Jeremiah Wright, who expounded revolutionary ideas. Ayers belatedly realized that books were better revolutionary tools than bombs and became a professor of education at the University of Illinois Chicago, where he advanced critical pedagogy further. Ayers is now retired but appears to remain a political radical. Obama long has been coy about acknowledging these relationships for easily understandable reasons given the longstanding and still considerable but diminishing American resistance to ideas and relationships identified as Marxist or communist. Indeed, Marxists have long hidden or misrepresented their political convictions to avoid alienating non-believers. For similar reasons, DEI advocates have developed the subterfuge that DEI is about "progressives" seeking "social justice."

Biden, of course, was Obama's vice president. The Biden White House has many veterans of Obama's White House staff. Biden's own vice president, Kamala Harris, who replaced him as the Democratic presidential candidate in 2024, was chosen to be his running mate specifically because she is a black woman.

The emphasis on identity groups rather than individuals enabled the Obama and Biden administrations to alter the political complexion of the federal workforce without violating the Civil Service Reform Act of 1978, which prohibits agencies from asking employees or applicants about their political views. Relying on polling data about the political views of narrowly defined demographic groups and the law of large numbers, Obama's administrators changed the political orientation of the workforce by hiring more people from groups with political views similar to his own under the rubric of social justice and DEI, not by packing the bureaucracy

---

[28] Paul Kengor, *The Communist: Frank Marshall Davis: The Untold Story of Barack Obama's Mentor* (Dallas TX: Mercury Ink, 2021).

with self-declared Democrats. Individuals chosen in this way could help advance his agenda through their supportive implementation of his policies; by "independently" interpreting laws, writing regulations, and making enforcement decisions consistent with his perspectives; and by allocating appropriations to favored organizations and purposes based on congenial ideological foundations.[29] Hiring persons of the so-called "Obama coalition" was advantageous in another attractive way—his political allies got jobs that helped cement their loyalty.

Unsurprisingly, critics soon began to claim that efforts designed to help allegedly "disadvantaged" or "underserved" groups were in fact another form of discrimination that not only was ethically unfair, but was harmful to the performance of government in general, and the IC in particular, by hiring, promoting, and assigning persons less qualified than healthy, heterosexual men of European origin.[30] This in turn soon produced the counter-claims expressed commonly by Obama administration officials such as DNI Clapper—that demographic diversity allegedly improves the operational performance of the IC. Biden's administration has maintained the Obama line while continuing to promote and expand DEI. In February 2021, for example, the Biden State Department created an "Office of Diversity and Inclusion" to implement DEI throughout the matrix of American diplomacy.

ODNI policies and guidance

DNIs, the senior U.S. intelligence officers since 2004, implement presidential guidance regarding many topics, including DEI. Some of them have developed and worked strenuously to embed IC-specific DEI policies first in the ODNI, then more broadly throughout the IC. What are now chief diversity officers at the ODNI gradually changed titles and roles and accumulated progressively more administrative power. Given DNIs' lack of significant executive power over the agencies, as specified by the intelligence reform act of 2004 that created the DNI position, the job is

---

[29] Mitch McConnell, "Liberal Bureaucrats Threaten Democracy," *Wall Street Journal*, June 12, 2024, A17; Rael Jean Isaac and Erich Isaac, *The Coercive Utopians: Social Deception by America's Power Players* (Chicago: Regnery Gateway, 1983), 221-250.
[30] Gentry, "Demographic Diversity in U.S. Intelligence Personnel."

often described as one of "herding cats."[31] Nevertheless, DNIs have some power, and they increasingly exercise it in DEI matters, often by delegating some of their authorities to their chief diversity officers.

Development of the power of chief diversity officers and their offices occurred over a relatively short period of time. In early 2006, the first DNI, John Negroponte, appointed the first Chief of Equal Employment Opportunity (EEO) for the IC and soon thereafter merged this office with the IC Diversity Strategies Division (formerly in the IC Chief Human Capital Office) to integrate EEO and diversity functions and leverage resources.[32] The Office of IC EEO and Diversity (EEOD) and its renamed successors have always been senior-level offices that report directly to the DNI. They regularly issue policy documents reflecting DNIs' command emphasis and authority.

In July 2009, Obama's first DNI, retired Admiral Dennis Blair (2009-2010), issued Intelligence Community Directive 110, "Equal Employment Opportunity and Diversity," which introduced the new concept of demographic rather than intellectual diversity to the IC and anticipated Obama's EO 13583 of 2011.[33] This ICD seems to mark the end of the EEO era in the IC; the term rarely appears in ODNI documents published thereafter. Blair said nothing about how DEI policies would affect the IC's performance, beginning an enduring tradition. According to former DCIA Leon Panetta (2009-2011), Obama's White House staffers tightly controlled the policies and activities of agency heads, including himself as CIA director, making clear that Obama drove Panetta's diversity initiatives.[34] Presumably Blair was similarly pressured.

DNI James Clapper

Blair was forced out in May 2010 after losing a power struggle with Panetta over control of CIA's field operatives. Obama's DEI effort in the IC accelerated under his second and final DNI, retired Air Force

---

[31] Author's personal experience. See also Brennan, *Undaunted*, 165-166.

[32] ODNI, "Diversity & Inclusion," n.d., https://www.dni.gov/index.php/how-we-work/diversity.

[33] Blair, ICD 110, https://www.dni.gov/files/documents/ICD/ICD_110.pdf.

[34] Leon Panetta with Jim Newton, *Worthy Fights: A Memoir of Leadership in War and Peace* (New York: Penguin, 2014), 232.

Lieutenant General James Clapper (2010-2017). Clapper made many changes in policies and took implementing actions to push DEI, first within the ODNI and then more broadly in the IC. Clapper formed two diversity offices in the ODNI. One addresses DEI issues within the ODNI alone. The other, more important office issues DEI policy guidance and monitors compliance in the IC as a whole. Clapper became overtly political in a partisan way immediately after he left office in January 2017, linking Obama and DEI closely to his partisanship. In this way he also violated two longstanding, very useful professional norms: former senior military and intelligence officers should not engage in partisan politics lest their activism reflect on the institutions in which they formerly served.[35]

Among his important DEI-related policy initiatives, in 2014 Clapper sought to engineer politically relevant changes to the organizational cultures of IC agencies by issuing a seven-part "Principles of Professional Ethics," with which he expected all IC employees to comply. One of the principles was and remains:

> DIVERSITY. We embrace the diversity of our nation, promote diversity and inclusion in our workforce, and encourage diversity in our thinking.[36]

Note that diversity of "thinking," which once was a priority because it is operationally useful, appears after demographic diversity—an ordering few experienced intelligence officers will miss given the preferred IC writing convention known as BLUF—Bottom Line Up Front. That is, key points in intelligence documents are to be put at the beginning of messages. In recent years, the principle increasingly might be seen as encouraging DEI orthodoxy per Obama in employees' thinking. Hence, there are now two ways to read "encourage diversity in our thinking."

---

[35] Jeff Rogg, "The U.S. Intelligence Community's 'MacArthur Moment,'" *International Journal of Intelligence and CounterIntelligence* 33:4 (2020): 666-681; John A. Gentry, "Trump-Era Politicization: A Code of Civil–Intelligence Behavior Is Needed," *International Journal of Intelligence and CounterIntelligence* 34:4 (2021): 757-786; Peter S. Usowski, "Former CIA Officers Writing about Intelligence, Policy, and Politics, 2016-2017," *Studies in Intelligence* 62:3 (Extracts, September 2018): 1-14.
[36] Principles, https://www.dni.gov/index.php/how-we-work/ethics.

Clapper clearly intended to push Obama's goal of making the IC "look like America."

The DEI policy priority, and IC "principle," entered later ODNI policy documents in the Obama years and remains in them. For example, Clapper added diversity to *National Intelligence Strategy* documents, which are modestly binding on IC agencies. Beginning with its 2014 iteration, the *Strategy* documents include Obama's "diversity and inclusion" mantra.[37] Clapper's Principles of Professional Ethics are prominently included in each *Strategy*, which ostensibly requires all intelligence officers to embrace and advance Obama's "diversity and inclusion" agenda. In 2015, Clapper issued a new *IC Equal Employment Opportunity and Diversity Enterprise Strategy, 2015-2020*, which set the strategic direction for numerous DEI-related initiatives across the community.[38] Senior executives of all IC agencies were held accountable through performance plan objectives that required them to describe how they were creating a more "inclusive" organizational culture. All senior executives were also required to complete "unconscious bias" training, which remains a requirement despite appreciable skepticism about its effectiveness.[39] "Unconscious bias" training has been administered to managers at CIA since the 1990s, at latest, where it generated much animosity and backlash, arguably rendering it counterproductive.[40] According to personal accounts, aggressive black "teachers" routinely race-bait white managers, ostensibly to tell them what it is like to be black—a tactic that still does not work well.

Clapper strongly supported and advocated for LGBTQ+ employees. After supporting gays earlier as director of the Defense Intelligence Agency (DIA) (1992-1995) and the National Geospatial-Intelligence Agency (2001-2006)—as DNI he spoke at government-funded conferences of what were then called "LGBT" people and wrote that he

---

[37] Director of National Intelligence, *National Intelligence Strategy, 2014*, 3.
[38] ODNI website, https://www.dni.gov/files/documents/Newsroom/Press%20Releases/2016EnterpriseStrategy.pdf.
[39] Christine Ro, "The complicated battle over unconscious bias training," BBC, March 28, 2021, https://www.bbc.com/worklife/article/20210326-the-complicated-battle-over-unconscious-bias-training.
[40] Multiple private communications with author.

was "proud" that gays had established an interagency "fly team" to help other LGBTQ+ people employed by IC agencies come out.[41] Clapper called Obama's 2015 decision to allow gays to serve openly in the military a "courageous act."[42] His assertion that increased numbers of LGBTQ+ personnel in the IC were good because they "brought unique perspectives to mission challenges and contributed to successes" was as close as he ever came to explaining how privileged identity groups help IC agencies perform better.[43] Clapper's Principal Deputy DNI, Stephanie O'Sullivan, the IC's second ranking official, hosted the first IC-wide event specifically designed to recruit LGBTQ+ persons in 2016.[44] Although Clapper had limited formal executive powers over the IC's agencies, some policies such as the *Strategy* documents and demonstrations like the LGBTQ+ recruiting event were important prods to the reconstruction of cultures in receptive agencies, most prominently the CIA, where he had an enthusiastic ally in director Brennan.[45]

In 2016, Clapper declared that he was unhappy with the results of his diversity promotion campaign. Despite his efforts, he proclaimed, the IC's proportions of women and minorities were below those of the rest of the federal workforce—his quantitative standard of comparison.[46] He therefore directed the ODNI's IC-oriented diversity chief, Rita Sampson, to publish the IC's diversity numbers in an unclassified format, in order to "hold us—*and more importantly, future leaders*—accountable for our shortcomings" (emphasis added).[47] In this and other ways, Clapper clearly intended to make permanent changes in the IC's demography, processes,

---

[41] Clapper, *Facts and Fears*, 262, 302.

[42] Ibid., 124.

[43] Ibid., 301.

[44] Mark Rosenball, "U.S. spy agencies to celebrate LGBT employees," *Reuters*, March 11, 2016, https://www.reuters.com/article/us-usa-spies-lgbt-idUSKCN0WD2EI.

[45] Ibid.; Brennan, *Undaunted*, 291. See also Susan M. Gordon, "CIA critics are making a false choice between diversity and excellence," *Washington Post*, May 11, 2021, Opinion | Susan Gordon: CIA critics are creating a false choice between diversity and excellence - The Washington Post.

[46] Nicole Ogrysko, "Why the intelligence community declassified its demographics stats for the first time," *Federal News Network*, June 13, 2016, https://federalnewsnetwork.com/hiring-retention/2016/06/intelligence-community-declassified-demographics-stats-first-time/.

[47] Clapper, *Facts and Fears*, 302.

and organizational culture that future administrations could not reverse. Limited anecdotal reporting consistent with published reports of similar Biden administration-wide efforts[48] indicates that DNI Avril Haines (2021-present), beginning in early 2024 at the latest, convened working groups tasked with taking steps to help ensure that another president, elected in 2024 or later, could not reverse Biden's (and her) changes in the IC.[49] This, too, arguably amounts to an effort to interfere with normal practices of American presidential transitions and could be called, in contemporary parlance, a "threat to democracy." But despite Clapper's pessimism, the report shows gains in employment for privileged identity groups. As always, it contains no statement about what level or kind of diversity is adequate or when adequacy might be achieved.[50] More is always better, seemingly forever.

Trump's DNIs

In contrast, President Trump's DNIs paid little attention to DEI issues. Clapper's policies remained in effect. According to journalist Bob Woodward, DNI Dan Coats (2017-2019) was initially overwhelmed by the workload and chose to focus on dealing with the president, Congress, and other external matters as a "Mr. Outside," leaving day-to-day management of the internal workings of the IC to "Mrs. Inside," Principal Deputy DNI Sue Gordon (2017-2019).[51] Gordon had thrived bureaucratically as a CIA officer in the Brennan years and evidently shared Brennan's demographic ambitions; she certainly indicated as much after leaving office. Hence, Coats did not try to reform DEI policies or the diversity offices of the ODNI or CIA that had become power bases of senior-level advocates for diversity and inclusion policies and intellectual bases of intelligence officers' partisan activism against Trump.[52] Nor did

---

[48] Betsy Klein and Tami Luhby, "Biden administration bolsters protections for federal workers, getting ahead of potential Trump moves," CNN, April 5, 2024, https://www.cnn.com/2024/04/04/politics/rule-protecting-federal-workers/index.html.

[49] Personal communication, 2024.

[50] ODNI, Diversity Report.

[51] Bob Woodward, *Rage* (New York: Simon & Schuster, 2020), 68-69; Gordon, "CIA critics are making a false choice between diversity and excellence."

[52] Gentry, *Neutering the CIA*, 329-360.

acting DNI Joseph Maguire (2019-2020), acting DNI Richard Grenell (2020), or DNI John Ratcliffe (2020-2021) roll back any Obama-era diversity policies. For example, the 2019 version of the *National Intelligence Strategy,* published well after Trump became president, is very similar to Clapper's 2014 version, making clear in another of many ways that the ODNI bureaucracy Clapper built had accepted and internalized Obama's DEI agenda.[53]

DNI Avril Haines

DNI Haines arguably was herself a DEI hire. A lawyer and veteran of the Obama White House staff, she was deputy DCIA to John Brennan for about a year and a half in 2013-2015—her only previous intelligence experience. In May 2023, Haines issued ICD 125, "Gender Identity and Inclusivity in the Intelligence Community."[54] This ICD makes the ODNI's DEIA officer responsible for implementing the policy and requires all IC personnel to take training on transgender issues annually in addition to the diversity-related courses previously required.

According to its website, the ODNI diversity officer is now active in furthering Biden's DEIA agenda. In mid-2024, the incumbent was Stephanie La Rue, a lawyer, former CIA officer, and career human resources specialist.[55] An ODNI journal called *The Dive*, initiated in 2023 on La Rue's watch, provides DEIA-focused guidance on thoughts, actions, and use of language to the IC as a whole—from senior managers to junior employees. Published initially at the For Official Use Only-level, one issue was declassified after a Freedom of Information Act request and released with a considerable number of redactions. It then was posted on the ODNI's public website.[56]

---

[53] ODNI, *National Intelligence Strategy, 2019*, https://www.dni.gov/index.php/newsroom/reports-publications/reports-publications-2019/3289-2019-national-intelligence-strategy.

[54] ICD 125, https://www.dni.gov/files/documents/ICD/ICD_125-Gender-Identity-and-Inclusivity.pdf.

[55] ODNI website, https://www.dni.gov/index.php/who-we-are/organizations/339-about/organization/diversity-equity-and-inclusion.

[56] ODNI, *The Dive*, https://www.dni.gov/files/documents/FOIA/DF-2024-00143-Dive-Winter-23-24.pdf.

Employees surely see this as a source of ideological orthodoxy to be imitated. Most intelligence people are bright, and they know how to divine meaning from hints and tones of communicated messages of various sorts, meaning not much nuance is required to pass such messages. Indeed, discerning nuances in the words and actions of foreign actors is a key professional skill for many intelligence officers, who also are keenly sensitive even to subtle messages emanating from their own senior officials because these de facto incentives affect their careers. For analysts, for example, passing their written products quickly and with modest changes through the "review process" of editorial review is key to job satisfaction and a successful career.[57] Analysts know that avoidance of offensive ideas or language will help get their drafts approved by senior managers who, they further know, have their own sets of DEI-related incentives. All experienced employees know, too, that senior managers tend to promote people with similar political views into senior positions, thereby replicating themselves and expanding their horizon of influence. Therefore, ambitious bureaucrats, like ambitious people everywhere, usually seek to please the bosses who can promote them.

The Dive issue affects these processes by telling IC personnel how to address DEI-related issues. Articles in *The Dive* are not subtle. The lead article presents, in essence, DEIA orthodoxy on use of language. Arguing that "words have power," it lists words to avoid. For example, it labels terms such as "blacklisted," "brown bag," "cakewalk," "grandfathered," and "sanity check" as offensive to privileged identity groups.[58] *The Dive* pointedly seeks to banish words and concepts allegedly offensive to black Americans, people who live in Africa, Muslims, the elderly, and individuals with mental problems. *The Dive* takes specific aim at concepts of Islam that might offend Muslim employees of the IC in ways that have analytic importance, a bias that evidently has already had analytic implications, as discussed below.

Other articles variously state favored and prohibited concepts, and articles serially cover privileged demographic identity groups to be sure to

---

[57] Gentry, "Managers of Analysts."
[58] ODNI, *The Dive*, Winter 23/24, 6-8.

embrace, or at least to avoid alienating. These stories play to the parochial concerns of the confederation of DEIA interest groups.

An anonymous male employee discussed his experiences as an occasional crossdresser in an article titled "My Gender Identity and Expression Make Me a Better Intelligence Officer." He writes, "I think my experiences as someone who crossdresses have sharpened the skills I use as an intelligence officer, particularly critical thinking and perspective-taking."[59] It helps, this fellow says, to know how uncomfortable women are when they wear high heels. Like Clapper's verbiage, this standard argument of the LGBTQ+ community and now the IC is especially tenuous. We know, because many have since "come out," that many gays served in the IC long before President Bill Clinton lifted the ban on homosexuals serving in 1995.[60] Previously, the concern was that gays were vulnerable to blackmail, making them counterintelligence risks. This concern was legitimate. Soviet intelligence regularly targeted and recruited gay people as agents, often through use of blackmail. The "Lavender Scare" of the 1950s and 1960s led to the dismissal of many gay federal employees over such security concerns. Gays who stayed "in the closet" often had successful careers precisely because their performance did *not* reflect the "unique perspectives" that Clapper and others have extolled.

In another article, a deaf employee writes approvingly of the help he or she received while on a deployment to Camp Lemonnier, Djibouti.[61] Given long working hours there on a six-month tour, the IC also deployed two sign-language interpreters to enable this person to communicate more easily with colleagues. The IC thus provided one intelligence officer for the price of three. Praising the IC's efforts to ensure accessibility, the article does not address the issue of cost-effectiveness or resource management.

Another article discusses the Sixth Annual Leadership Summit of the African American Affinity Network (AAAN) and the Latino Intelligence

---

[59] Ibid., 10.
[60] CIA, no byline, "Employee Group Received Award for Promoting LGBT Issues," December 16, 2016, https://www.cia.gov/stories/story/cia-employee-group-receives-award-for-promoting-lgbt-issues/.
[61] ODNI, *The Dive*, Winter 23/24, 12-13.

Network (LINK), two of the IC agencies' dozen or so "affinity groups" that focus on the interests of their specific racial/ethnic/gender group.[62] The meeting, held on September 6-7, 2023, at the ODNI's Bethesda, Maryland, campus, featured an ODNI DEIA presentation on the alleged "underrepresentation" of black and Hispanic personnel in the IC. In fact, as noted, blacks are proportionately represented in the IC but are substantially overrepresented in the federal work force as a whole.[63] Many Hispanics in the United States are not citizens, a firm IC requirement, do not speak English, and do not have skills useful to the IC. No matter. The emphasis again was on increasing the raw numbers of people from politically favored demographic identity groups and fostering intersectional alliances useful for advocating narrow demographic identity group interests, defined in this case as politically adequate hiring and promotion rates for group members.

In other initiatives, the ODNI's "Small Steps" program bolsters DEI.[64] This effort aims to encourage employees to accept some behavioral aspects of privileged groups' desires. These are small steps toward inclusiveness, it is argued. This program is administered throughout the IC. Much of the rest of government has similar programs. According to an informed government employee, the State Department-wide version of the program, including in its intelligence bureau, the Bureau of Intelligence and Research (INR), awards "points" to individuals and small work groups for doing things favored by privileged identity groups, such as listing pronouns on one's email signature block or attending workshops or training sessions on diversity-related subjects beyond those mandated by policy.[65] Each month, State holds an awards ceremony that honors persons and groups accumulating the most points. At one ceremony in 2023, Principal Deputy DNI Stacey Dixon presided.

The "Small Steps" program resembles the Chinese Communist Party's (CCP's) "social credit system," created coincidentally in 2014, when

---

[62] Ibid., 14.

[63] Office of the Director of National Intelligence, "Annual Demographic Report: Hiring and Retention of Minorities, Women, and Persons with Disabilities in the United States Intelligence Community Fiscal Year 2016," 46.

[64] The ODNI's web pages devoted to this program were down as of this writing.

[65] Personal communication, 2023.

Obama's resocialization efforts in the federal workforce were underway. The social credit system effectively groups Chinese citizens into three categories based on their compliance with CCP behavioral orthodoxies (and their interpretations by local authorities) in their daily lives.[66] Individuals who are especially ideologically diligent in their social lives get special perquisites, including good jobs and university educations for their children. Recalcitrant people are punished in various ways, such as by diminished job prospects and denial of access to high-speed transportation. Most Chinese evidently are in a middle category, receiving neither special benefits nor punishments. The national system, like Biden's DEIA regime, remains under development.

DEI policies at the intelligence agencies

Agency heads variously implement, and in some cases enhance, presidential and DNI diversity policies. Obama's first DCIA, Leon Panetta (2009-2011), told the CIA workforce in an unclassified internal memo in July 2009 that he would increase the presence of minorities in the CIA's staff from 22 percent at the time of the memo to 30 percent by 2012, a rapid increase given the agency's lengthy hiring process and low turnover rate.[67] This effort would help make the CIA "look like" America, Panetta averred.[68] No performance goals or implications were initially—or indeed ever—stated. This numeric target was evidently an interim goal. Like presidents and DNIs, no senior agency official has ever identified a threshold number or percentage of the workforce that would reach "enough" diversity. More hires and promotions of individuals from favored groups are always positive.

Per Obama's EO 13583, "diversity offices" in each federal agency establish and enforce accountability standards under which agencies and employees are punished for failure to comply with the order. Among intelligence agency directors, Brennan implemented the EO especially

---

[66] Bertelsmann-Stiftung, "China's Social Credit System," n.d., https://www. bertelsmann-stiftung.de/fileadmin/files/aam/Asia-Book_A_03_China_Social_ Credit_System.pdf.
[67] John A. Gentry, "Intelligence Learning and Adaptation: Lessons from Counterinsurgency Wars," *Intelligence and National Security* 25:1 (2010): 75.
[68] Ibid.

aggressively at the CIA. Brennan recounted in his memoirs that he long had been dissatisfied with certain aspects of CIA culture.[69] As he progressed in rank, he wrote, he took opportunities to change it. For example, as head of a team assessing analytic tradecraft in 1994, he relished "the ability to shape the Agency's analytic culture."[70] As DCIA, Brennan had many more opportunities to change the culture, working closely with "the inimitable Jim Clapper," who was his "foxhole buddy and good friend" as well as ideological comrade in working to reshape the IC's demography and organizational cultures.[71]

DCIA John Brennan

Brennan changed policies and structures, and thereby organizational incentives, in order to alter the CIA's organizational culture in ways that would be politically significant, operationally important, and enduring. In December 2013, he commissioned a study, eventually published in 2015 as *Director's Diversity in Leadership Study*, citing Obama's EO 13583 as the authority for his decision.[72] Prepared by a group chaired by civil rights activist and longtime Democratic adviser Vernon Jordan,[73] the *Study* claimed that "The Agency's workforce is not diverse."[74] This statement is flatly contradicted by figures in the report, but the study accurately reported that white males held a larger share of senior positions than junior ones. The study claimed, also without evidence, that more domestically defined demographic diversity was necessary to help the agency perform

---

[69] Brennan, *Undaunted*, 132, 140, 283, 270, 286.

[70] Ibid., 94.

[71] Ibid., 7, 414.

[72] John Brennan, "CIA Diversity and Inclusion Strategy (2016-2019)," 3, https://www.cia.gov/library/reports/Diversity_Inclusion_Strategy_2016_to_2019.pdf.

[73] Vernon's group consisted of Michèle Flournoy, Justin Jackson, Steve Kappes, retired Admiral Mike Mullen, and Catherine Pino. Flournoy was undersecretary of defense for policy in 2009-2012. Jackson, who said in a Washington radio interview that "We need more diversity," was the CIA's highest ranking black employee. Kappes was a senior CIA operations officer and deputy DCIA who resigned in controversial circumstances. Mullen, as chairman of the Joint Chiefs of Staff, was an outspoken proponent of racial diversity in high military ranks and supported ending the "don't ask, don't tell" policy regarding gays in the military. Pino is a lesbian activist and professional diversity consultant. This was not an intellectually diverse group.

[74] CIA website, https://www.cia.gov/library/reports/dls-report.pdf, 13.

better. Said Brennan: "CIA simply must do more to develop the diverse and inclusive leadership environment that our values require and that our mission demands." [75]

Brennan's diversity strategy for 2016-2019 contained a "roadmap" for boosting diversity.[76] Another formal "roadmap" plan still in effect in 2019 listed diversity and inclusion as one of its five goals.[77]

Brennan had a reputation for partisanship even before he became a political appointee. Former CIA operations officer Sam Faddis wrote, "John Brennan, CIA Director under President Obama, was technically an analyst, although his real profession for most of his career was being a Democratic political hack."[78] A retired CIA analyst less caustically reported that in the early 2000s Brennan had a reputation in parts of CIA for expressing outspokenly partisan, pro-Democratic Party views.[79] According to another former CIA officer, Brennan developed a reputation among CIA analysts for politicizing intelligence by giving President Obama what he wanted to hear, not objective analysis—a cardinal analytic sin under the old normative regime.[80] Former CIA and National Security Agency (NSA) director General Michael Hayden made the same point, albeit aimed less pointedly at Brennan, by saying the CIA politicized its products in the Brennan years by pandering to White House wishes on intelligence that partly enabled the Joint Comprehensive Plan of Action (JCPOA), the nuclear deal with Iran concluded in July 2015, and by initially discounting signs of Russian meddling in U.S. politics in deference to Obama's effort to "reset" relations with Russia.[81] Hayden claimed incongruously that the analysts were only committing "a subtle

---

[75] Adam B. Lerner, "CIA study: White men dominate agency's top ranks," *Politico*, June 30, 2015, https://www.politico.com/story/2015/06/cia-internal-study-white-men-dominate-agency-top-ranks-minorities-119603. See also Brennan, *Undaunted*, 289-290.

[76] CIA press release, https://www.cia.gov/stories/story/cia-releases-diversity-and-inclusion-strategy-for-2016-2019/.

[77] CIA presentation to former employees, summer 2019.

[78] Charles "Sam" Faddis, "We Are Late," June 25, 2019, http://andmagazine.com/talk/2019/06/25/we-are-late/.

[79] Personal conversation, early 2019.

[80] Private communication with a retired senior CIA analyst, 2019.

[81] Michael V. Hayden, *The Assault on Intelligence: American National Security in an Age of Lies* (New York: Penguin, 2018), 36-37.

form of self-censorship" or "self-policing," not politicization.[82] This distinction is nonsense; it is a classic case of the politicization of intelligence of the sort Sherman Kent warned about in 1949, and which long was taboo at the CIA.[83] Retired operations officer Douglas London, who says he dealt periodically with Brennan as DCIA, went further, arguing that Brennan politicized CIA intelligence generally in intended support of Obama and his foreign policies.[84]

These partisan political traits were evident in the DEI arena. Brennan actively participated in events within the CIA that celebrated Obama's privileged identity groups—minorities, LGBTQ+ individuals, and women.[85] Disabled people were not yet a major priority. After Brennan spoke to a group of black intelligence personnel at the National Security Executives and Professionals Association's Third Annual National Security and Intelligence Career Development and Leadership Summit on May 21, 2016, the group's president Reginald King cited Brennan's efforts to bring blacks into the CIA and said "Mr. Brennan has taken the conversation about diversity and inclusion further than it has ever been taken in my 26 years with the Agency."[86] The group's conventions, unsurprisingly, began during the Obama years.

Brennan clearly understood that creation of incentives—positive and negative—is often the best way to motivate and shape bureaucratic behavior.[87] As noted, CIA officers are typically savvy in the political sense that they accurately read even modest bureaucratic signals as de facto instructions. Brennan's DEI-related incentives permeated the agency. Citing the *Director's Diversity in Leadership Study*, he made clear that he would hold managers personally accountable for increasing "diversity," defined narrowly in domestically relevant demographic terms. While there evidently are no publicly reported cases in which Brennan personally

---

[82] Ibid.

[83] Kent, *Strategic Intelligence for American World.*

[84] Douglas London, *The Recruiter: Spying and the Lost Art of American Intelligence* (New York: Hachette, 2021), 376-382.

[85] Brennan, *Undaunted*, 291.

[86] CIA, "Director Brennan Speaks at NSEPA Conference," CIA website, https://www.cia.gov/news-information/featured-story-archive/2016-featured-story-archive/director-brennan-speaks-at-nsepa-conference.html.

[87] Gentry, "Managers of Analysts."

punished a manager for a failure in this arena, more junior managers surely did so. For example, a now retired person then working in CIA's Directorate of Support said her managers punished subordinates who did not support Brennan's diversity policies.[88] She quietly opposed the policies and stated explicitly that she felt intimidated.[89]

Brennan used his position to influence the CIA's culture in even superficial ways—such as wearing a rainbow lanyard (which holds employees' identification documents) in deference to LGBTQ+ employees—which by many accounts was soon mimicked by his immediate subordinates, and then theirs.[90] Previously, employees wore plain lanyards or chains or lanyards that expressed support for favorite sports teams, but never lanyards that expressed politically sensitive messages. Another unsubtle indicator of command emphasis was internalized. Another useful norm was jettisoned. The structural, policy, and cultural changes that Brennan instituted, only modest need to punish recalcitrant managers, and ODNI figures showing "progress" in re-shaping the demographics of the CIA workforce suggest that Brennan generally got his way. Still, Brennan claimed in his memoirs that some employees told him pointedly that they opposed his diversity policies and others.[91] He evidently ignored them.

By many accounts, Brennan successfully used DEI-related policies and incentives to alter the organizational cultures of the CIA in politically relevant ways. The evidence also strongly suggests that this social and demographic engineering contributed to the unprecedented outburst of political activism from current and former intelligence officers directed at candidate and then President Donald J. Trump, which surfaced only when Trump appeared to become a viable threat to Obama's DEI policies in the summer of 2016.[92] Former CIA analyst and manager Nicholas Dujmović believes Obama generated "rock star hero worship" in many CIA

---

[88] Ibid.
[89] Personal communication, 2022.
[90] Brennan, *Undaunted,* 290.
[91] Ibid., 283, 290, 295-296, 299-300.
[92] Gentry, *Neutering the CIA,* 231-328.

employees, especially younger people hired in large numbers after 2001.[93] Another former CIA officer said there was "a lot of sub rosa support for Obama" during the 2008 election campaign.[94] Former DCIA Michael Hayden agreed that intelligence people generally held a "positive" view of Obama.[95] Despite some tensions over such issues as the CIA's use of controversial interrogation methods on terrorism suspects during the George W. Bush years, widespread affection for Obama was both personal and political—sharply different from their feelings about Trump. Obama, Clapper, and Brennan successfully changed the CIA's culture and appealed to many employees for whom DEI policies were both ideologically congenial and materially beneficial. In early 2016, there was no need for employee concerns about Trump because, like most pollsters, they expected Hillary Clinton to win the presidency in 2016 and continue Obama's policies. Many sources indicate that it was Trump's emergence as a serious threat to Clinton in mid-2016, and thence potentially to the DEI policies many of them favored, that led to overt activism against Trump among former and current CIA personnel.[96] Thereafter, some IC people, most obviously including former FBI director James Comey, who stated publicly that he hoped to induce Trump's impeachment and removal from office, actively sought to undermine Trump's presidency.

Brennan explicitly encouraged such activism after Trump was elected—while he was DCIA—using DEI policies as a prod. Soon after Trump's election, Brennan reported in his memoir, "a significant number" of female, Muslim, black, and LGBTQ+ employees expressed to him their concerns that Trump's comments portended a possible retreat from the agency's diversity and inclusion regime.[97] In response, he and deputy DCIA David Cohen held two meetings with employees in the agency's auditorium. Brennan recalled saying, "Do not let the progress be undone … You know what is right. If you see that a colleague is not being treated fairly, speak up. If you believe that Agency leaders are not fulfilling their

---

[93] Author discussion with Nicholas Dujmović, June 19, 2019; Panetta, *Worthy Fights*, 221.
[94] Personal communication, 2019.
[95] Hayden, *Assault on Intelligence*, 33-38.
[96] Gentry, *Neutering the CIA*.
[97] Brennan, *Undaunted*, 392.

responsibilities to promote diversity and inclusion, speak out. You have the ability to shape the Agency's future. Seize it, and never let it go."[98]

Brennan thereby encouraged CIA employees to emulate and support his activist political agenda, focusing especially on DEI policies. Soon thereafter, he told a reporter that he met with the CIA workforce several times before his departure from office to tell them that while the agency's progress on diversity and inclusion over the years had been significant, it was their responsibility to keep it moving forward. The reporter recounted Brennan's claim to have said: "It's up to you to make sure it's not going to be reversible … If [you] see something that is wrong or not in keeping with the agency's commitment to diversity and inclusion … [you] need to speak up and speak out."[99]

In other words Brennan, like Clapper at the ODNI, told CIA personnel to participate overtly in political activities, internally or externally, in ways that were ideologically motivated and designed to thwart the freedom of action of his duly appointed successors. He came even closer than Clapper to explicitly calling for insubordination against Trump while still a government official. Later, as a retiree no longer subject to the Hatch Act of 1939, which prohibits government employees from participating in partisan politics, he did so explicitly by telling an MSNBC audience that FBI employees should "not follow" presidential orders related to a 2019 Justice Department investigation into whether the FBI, and other IC personnel, including himself, acted improperly in prompting or supporting the probe of Russian connections to the 2016 Trump campaign.[100]

It was a radically different approach from that any other DCIA or director of central intelligence had taken before him. It also was inappropriate given the normative prohibition on overt communication of political views both inside and outside CIA by serving intelligence

---

[98] Ibid., 392-393.

[99] Jenna McLaughlin, "More White, More Male, More Jesus: CIA Employees Fear Pompeo Is Quietly Killing the Agency's Diversity Mandate," *Foreign Policy*, September 7, 2017, https://foreignpolicy.com/2017/09/08/more-white-more-male-more-jesus-cia-employees-fear-pompeo-is-quietly-killing-the-agencys-diversity-mandate/.

[100] No byline, "Brennan: FBI Officials 'Have an Obligation' to 'Not Follow' Trump's Declassification Order," *Grabien News*, September 18, 2018, https://grabien.com/story.php?id=194013.

officers. But given that many employees evidently agreed with his philosophy and policies, and that evolving societal norms permitted freer expression of personal political opinions, Brennan's last words as DCIA probably gave a modest additional spur to the political activism by employees, which blossomed after Trump's election. An exhortation by a senior sitting official presumably helped some CIA employees convince themselves that their political activism was sanctioned, legitimate, and acceptable.

Cindy Otis, a manager of analysts during Brennan's years as director, confirmed his influence. Otis wrote a strident op-ed against President Trump in 2018, claiming that she acted in accordance with Brennan's regular advice to CIA personnel to speak "truth to power" in defense of policies he favored.[101] In the context of Trump's then-controversial but eventually unfulfilled threat to revoke Brennan's security clearance, Otis wrote:

> In John Brennan's last address to employees as CIA director, he told us he planned to slip quietly into civilian life when he left. He also repeated two things that were always key points of all his talks with employees: that the work CIA employees do is critical to protecting the country, and that officers have a responsibility to speak the truth.
>
> Trump's retaliation against Brennan is sadly not unexpected given the president's almost daily insults against perceived opponents over Twitter, the war he continues to wage against our constitutional rights to a free press and free speech, and his disdain for the intelligence community. It is more important than ever

---

[101] "Truth to power" is a slogan that developed in the 1960s at the CIA and has reemerged periodically since when CIA personnel opposed presidents. It conveys the message that CIA employees know "the truth" and that they therefore have an obligation to try to thwart presidential powers they do not like. It was used extensively against Trump. See John A. Gentry, "'Truth' as a Tool of the Politicization of Intelligence," *International Journal of Intelligence and CounterIntelligence* 32:2 (2019): 217-247.

before that national security professionals speak truth to power, as Brennan has long advocated.[102]

Brennan told the *Wall Street Journal* in January 2017, just before leaving office, that he hoped he would be remembered most for the "way he fought to nurture a workforce that reflected America's diversity."[103] This is a strong statement of his determination to impose a new domestic politics-oriented regime on the CIA. In sharp contrast, soon-to-be-former intelligence leaders after nearly four years on the job usually cite major accomplishments in the operational performance of their organizations. Not Brennan.

Brennan successfully institutionalized Obama's "diversity and inclusion" agenda in a major IC agency. As former CIA manager Nicholas Dujmović noted, Brennan created at the CIA what many analysts called a form of ideology-driven "soft totalitarianism"—as opposed to the "hard" totalitarianism of the Soviet Union and China—enforced by the diversity offices, which focused on advancing "progress" in the social arenas, especially guided by DEI.[104] He also left an action plan and a staff at the CIA to continue his politically-oriented work after he left office.[105] As noted, Sue Gordon as Principal Deputy DNI was effectively the chief operating officer of the ODNI for most of Trump's four years in office, given DNI Coats' decision to focus on external matters. As at the ODNI, "The team implementing the CIA's efforts to build a diverse workforce, which is led by a senior Agency officer dedicated to this task, is still in

---

[102] Cindy Otis, "What Trump did to Brennan recalls authoritarians I studied at the CIA," *USA Today*, August 16, 2018, https://www.usatoday.com/story/opinion/2018/08/16/trump-brennan-national-security-clearance-recalls-authoritarians-studied-cia-column/1006752002/.

[103] Shane Harris, "CIA Director John Brennan Rejects Donald Trump's Criticism," *Wall Street Journal*, January 16, 2017, https://www.wsj.com/articles/cia-director-john-brennan-rejects-donald-trumps-criticism-1484611514.

[104] This term seems to have been used frequently at the CIA before Heather Mac Donald cited it. See Mac Donald, *The Diversity Delusion: How Race and Gender Pandering Corrupt the University and Undermine Our Culture* (New York: St. Martin's, 2018), 28.

[105] No byline or date, "20 Years of Pride," Central Intelligence Agency, https://www.cia.gov/news-information/featured-story-archive/2016-featured-story-archive/20-years-of-pride.html.

place and working on these efforts. See our website which continues to publish that strategy," a CIA spokesperson said in September 2017, when Trump was president.[106] Another CIA spokesperson said virtually the same in July 2019.[107]

In the Obama years, among IC agency heads only the CIA's Brennan strenuously pushed Obama's DEI agenda. Other heads maintained largely traditional policies while adopting some of Obama's agenda as embedded in EO 13583.[108] That would change dramatically in the Biden years, following the intervening administration of Donald J. Trump.

Trump's CIA directors

Just as Trump's DNIs did nothing to reverse Obama-era DEI policies, his CIA directors also did nothing, and in one way modestly expanded Obama's program. DCIA Mike Pompeo (2017-2018) was director for 15 months. By many accounts he changed little; he was still learning the job. But he was immediately chastised by employees for not displaying Brennan's enthusiasm for DEI. For example, after his first address to the CIA workforce in the agency's auditorium, employees repeatedly asked Pompeo about his commitment to Brennan's diversity program. After the third question on that theme, he said he was committed to finding the best people for jobs—the traditional standard—which was plainly unacceptable to some people in attendance.[109] Said one employee who heard Pompeo speak, "He didn't seem to understand the need for a workforce that reflects America."[110] Former CIA analyst Ned Price, an openly gay officer who served a rotational tour in Obama's White House while working for the CIA and was later Biden's State Department spokesperson, remarked in mid-2019 that he still saw a need for the CIA to "resemble the country we protect"—a domestic political imperative that

---

[106] Ibid.

[107] Author's communication with this official at a CIA briefing event, July 25, 2019.

[108] Gentry, *Neutering the CIA*, 109-200.

[109] John Kiriakou, "Mike Pompeo's CIA Will Not Reflect America's Diversity," *truthdig*, September, 17, 2017, https://www.truthdig.com/articles/mike-pompeos-cia-will-not-reflect-america/.

[110] Ibid.

was not an operational motive or a desire to ensure equal opportunities for all, but an ideological view popular at the CIA in the Brennan years.[111]

A practicing Christian, Pompeo received much overt criticism from LGBTQ+ employees because he did not embrace them the way Brennan had. Price, for example, criticized Pompeo for allegedly trying to "impose his worldview on a workforce that values diversity as a strength."[112] As evidence, Price cited Pompeo's frustration with questions about diversity at the all-hands meeting described above, his alteration of and failure to attend the CIA's 2017 Pride Month ceremonies, and his consultation with the Family Research Council, a Christian organization that Price called an "anti-gay hate group," regarding an initiative to expand the CIA's chaplaincy program. Later, some CIA employees almost mindlessly criticized Pompeo's wife Susan, who was honorary chair of the CIA's Family Advisory Board, a group that addresses employee quality-of-life issues—an innocuous but modestly helpful role.[113] This criticism was not confined to the agency. When Trump nominated Pompeo to become Secretary of State in 2018, Price publicly denounced him in an error-ridden screed published in *Foreign Policy*.[114] Still, Pompeo did not change any Brennan-era DEI policies, which remained the norm throughout the Trump years.

Trump's second and final DCIA, Gina Haspel (2018-2021), also did not rock the DEI boat. A more traditional CIA careerist than Brennan, she was strongly inclined to go with the flow of existing CIA policies and practices, which by her time as director was the entrenched DEI regime. She made headlines by naming women to most of CIA's senior positions soon after she became director, creating what some pundits called a

---

[111] Ned Price discussion with author, July 30, 2019.

[112] Ned Price, "Good Riddance to CIA Director Pompeo," *Foreign Policy*, March 16, 2018, https://foreignpolicy.com/2018/03/16/good-riddance-to-cia-director-pompeo/.

[113] Shane Harris, "Susan Pompeo's role as 'first lady of the CIA' draws critics and defenders," *Washington Post*, March 19, 2018, https://www.washingtonpost.com/world/national-security/susan-pompeos-role-as-first-lady-of-the-cia-draws-critics-and-defenders/2018/03/19/d6e55646-2baf-11e8-911f-ca7f68bff0fc_story.html.

[114] Price, "Good Riddance to CIA Director Pompeo." See also Gentry, *Neutering the CIA*, 267-269.

"sisterhood of spies."[115] Like Sue Gordon, Haspel had thrived bureaucratically in the Brennan years, when she was the London station chief, a plum assignment for an operations officer.[116] In March 2020, she issued a multiyear extension of Brennan's diversity and inclusion policy with little change.[117] While her introductory statement is traditional, emphasizing the operational advantages of diversity in perspectives, the body of the document recalled Brennan, reemphasizing the importance of diversity as defined in terms of the domestic demographic groups. Strategic goal 2.2 adds yet another domestic constituency to the list of politically favored groups at the CIA: individuals "identifying as neurodiverse,"[118] that is, people with cognitive disorders such as dyslexia and autism.

The ODNI and the agencies balkanized their workforces in the name of equity by creating what are variously known as "employee resource groups" or "affinity groups." In 2019, NSA had specified and given code names to eleven demographically defined "employee resource groups:"

- AA (African-American)
- AAPI (Asian-American/Pacific Islander)
- AIAN (American Indian/Alaska Native)
- AV (American Veteran)
- ESL (English as a Second Language)
- HLAT (Hispanic/Latino)
- IC (Islamic Culture)
- NG (Next Gen)
- PRIDE (Lesbian, Gay, Bisexual, Transgender & Allies)
- PWD (People with Disabilities)
- W (Women)[119]

---

[115] Bob Windrem, "Sisterhood of spies: Women now hold the top positions at the CIA," NBC News, January 5, 2019, https://www.nbcnews.com/news/us-news/all-three-cia-directorates-will-now-be-headed-women-n954956.

[116] Katrina Manson, "Gina Haspel, the undercover spy picked to head the CIA," *Financial Times*, March 18, 2018, https://www.ft.com/content/e1f2760a-27a3-11e8-b27e-cc62a39d57a0.

[117] CIA, "Diversity and Inclusion Strategy, 2020-2023," March 2020, https://www.cia.gov/library/reports/DI_Strategy_2020.pdf.

[118] Ibid., 5.

[119] NSA website, https://www.intelligence,gov/nsa/nsadiversity.html, as of August 5, 2019.

Eligibility for membership in these groups is based solely on demographic group identity, but others can volunteer to be "allies" of affinity groups—defined as "friends" or "supporters" of the group's members. Even some applicants for government jobs are now asked about group(s) with which they plan "to ally"—arguably a violation of the Civil Service Reform Act of 1978, which prohibits government workers from asking applicants about their political preferences.[120] Composed of demographic groups other than healthy, heterosexual men of European origin who are not military veterans, they are ostensibly designed to create "safe spaces," where supposedly "oppressed" people can find mutual support—and relief from alleged "microaggressions" or worse from white males. Supposedly a means to assist stressed employees, they are in fact models of longstanding cultural Marxist tactics—divide people into identity groups that emphasize group differences and assume implicitly or explicitly that a dominant group—white males in this case—is oppressive and that all other groups are its oppressed victims. An Asian-American veteran of the U.S. armed forces said that when he joined his agency's Asian-American affinity group, members told him he was expected to complain about the oppressors.[121] When he said that in fact he felt welcomed in America, he was chastised. Another Asian-American, who once worked for a major IC agency's diversity office, confirmed this was a purpose of the affinity groups.[122]

Affinity groups are designed to push their own interests and to avoid compromise. Teresa Horne,[123] a black woman who in 2024 was director of the Office of Diversity and Equal Opportunity at the Defense Counterintelligence and Security Agency, an intelligence-related organization that is not an IC member agency, made the point clearly in a recorded presentation of the Intelligence and National Security Alliance (INSA). Horne said her goal was to hire more black people—period—and that black employees of government agencies were under no obligation to

[120] Personal communication with an applicant to the FBI, 2023.
[121] Personal communication, 2023.
[122] Personal communication, 2022.
[123] Horne biography, at https://www.insaonline.org/detail-pages/person/theresa-horne.

"assimilate" with the agencies' other personnel.[124] It was the duty of the agencies to accept and reward distinctive cultural characteristics of black Americans, she said. Horne's personal website prominently uses the Marxist term "intersectionality."[125]

Blacks in Government (BIG), a self-described political advocacy organization and support group for African-Americans founded in 1975, was active in the IC in the Obama years and was especially prominent at DIA.[126] Within the CIA, black-only groups also included the "Black Executive Board" and the "Board Room."[127]

In my time at National Intelligence University (NIU) (2011-2015), virtually all decisions made by committees, as opposed to executive decisions, such as hiring decisions, had to have a person of sub-Saharan African descent on the committee. This pointed effort to inject race into even mundane administrative decision-making was a requirement of the DIA, which then was NIU's executive agent.

Biden's agency heads

As Biden's CIA director, William Burns (2021-present) is a firm supporter of Biden's DEIA policies. He regularly extols their virtues and continues Brennan-era hiring, promotion, award, and assignment policies. CIA's updated DEIA strategy for 2024-2027 contains introductory messages by him and CIA's Chief Diversity and Inclusion Officer Jerry Laurienti, who urge "each Directorate and Mission Center to adopt tailored implementation plans that allow our officers to enable mission with a DEIA focus."[128] This is clear guidance. The *conduct* of mission-related activities must reflect and enhance President Biden's DEIA agenda. DEIA must be embedded in the ways CIA does things, in its organizational

---

[124] INSA Session, "Cultivating and Retaining Diverse Talent," February 21, 2024, https://www.insaonline.org/detail-pages/event/past-event/2024/02/21/default-calendar/beyond-recruitment-cultivating-and-retaining-diverse-talent-in-national-security.
[125] Horne website, https://www.drtheresahorne.com.
[126] BIG website, http://www.bignet.org/.
[127] CIA, *Director's Diversity in Leadership Study*, 17, CIA website, https://www.cia.gov/library/reports/dls-report.pdf.
[128] CIA, "CIA Diversity, Equity, Inclusion, and Accessibility Strategy, 2024-2027," n.d., https://www.cia.gov/careers/static/e777bbb28cf1605c2021de62754a3714/DIO-Strategy_2024.pdf.

culture. This document indicates a close working relationship between Burns and his diversity office, consistent with structures across government and other types of organizations which require diversity officers to report directly to the highest level of management.[129]

Unlike in the Obama and Trump years, under Biden IC agencies other than the CIA showed clear signs of institutionalizing DEIA within their organizational cultures. Biden administration officials pushed DEIA harder than Obama's team did. The most obvious cases are those of the FBI under director Christopher Wray (2017-present), who was held over from the Trump administration, and the State Department under Antony Blinken (2021-present), an unabashed proponent of DEIA policies.

The FBI's diversity office was established in 2013 but was not very active in the Obama or Trump years.[130] Wray named the bureau's first chief diversity officer in 2021, after Biden became president. As Wray is quoted on the FBI's diversity website, "The diversity and inclusion of our workforce is something I care deeply about … because the success of our efforts impacts our operations, our culture, and our future."[131] For the FBI, unlike for the foreign-focused IC agencies, "looking like" America makes somewhat more sense because the FBI operates mainly in the United States and criminals come in all demographic varieties. But critics of the FBI's DEI policies, including many current and former FBI officials, believe Wray pushed DEIA for ideological, not soundly functional, reasons.[132]

Blinken appears to be even more enthusiastic. In February 2021, almost immediately after taking office, he announced the creation of a "Diversity and Inclusion Office" whose chief diversity and inclusion officer would report directly to him. The Office soon produced a "Diversity and Inclusion Strategic Plan" to guide the work of a "D&I

---

[129] The chief of the State Department's Office of Diversity and Inclusion, which was created in February 2021, reports directly to the Secretary of State, for example, while college and university diversity office chiefs typically report to their institutional presidents.
[130] National Alliance, "Report," 61.
[131] FBI Jobs website, https://fbijobs.gov/diversity.
[132] National Alliance, "Report."

Leadership Council."[133] Blinken said he would require each of the State Department's regional bureaus to designate a deputy assistant secretary to focus on creating more diversity and stated that his goal was "to incorporate diversity and inclusion into the department's work at every level."[134] Blinken cited racial statistics and claimed, as usual without supporting evidence or logic, that fostering DEIA policies is a "national security priority." On April 12, 2021, he named Ambassador Gina Abercrombie-Winstanley, a black foreign service officer, as the State Department's first chief diversity and inclusion officer.[135] Among other initiatives, Abercrombie-Winstanley advocated diminishing the importance of the Foreign Service's challenging written exam – the major merit-based element in hiring – and requiring all promotion seekers to describe how they had "advanced inclusion."[136] Her eventual successor Zakiya Carr Johnson, who took over in April 2024, is not a professional diplomat, but rather a black woman activist and diversity consultant who had been a State Department adviser and Congressional staffer specializing in diversity issues.[137] She is on the record calling America a "failed historical model" with a "colonizing past."[138] Hence, State under Biden "caught up" with the DEI agenda embraced in the Obama years at the ODNI and CIA.

---

[133] Nicole Gaouette, "Blinken says he aims to create a more diverse State Department," CNN, February 25, 2021, https://www.cnn.com/2021/02/24/politics/blinken-diversity-inclusion-chief-officer/index.html#:~:text=Secretary%20of%20State%20 Antony%20Blinken%20will%20launch%20a,diplomacy%20"stronger%2C%20smar ter%2C%20more%20creative%20and%20more%20innovative."

[134] Ibid.

[135] Antony Blinken remarks, April 12, 2021, https://www.state.gov/secretary-antony-j-blinken-at-the-announcement-of-ambassador-gina-abercrombie-winstanley-as-chief-diversity-and-inclusion-officer/.

[136] Gina Abercrombie-Winstanley, "Creating a Culture of Inclusion at State," *The Foreign Service Journal*, September 2020, https://afsa.org/creating-culture-inclusion-state.

[137] Paul du Quenoy, "The State Department Should Dump DEI," *Newsweek*, April 4, 2024.

[138] Hannah Grossman, "New State Department diversity chief believes US is a 'failed historical model' with a 'colonizing past,'" Fox, April 10, 2024, https://www.foxnews.com/media/new-state-department-diversity-chief-believes-us-failed-historic-model-colonizing-past?msockid=385134a428d9620d0707257f296e6306.

In the Biden years, DEIA policies spread throughout the IC, generating both support and opposition. DEIA generated significant opposition among current and former FBI officials. The FBI acted unusually aggressively against "whistleblowers," firing some and putting others on leave without pay status for extended periods of time, a hardship that may be purposefully inflicted to prevent dissidents from working (and earning) elsewhere without resigning.[139] DEI-related controversies at the FBI also generated much negative publicity for the bureau.[140]

Hiring and promotion policies

An explicit purpose of DEI policies is to hire more, and differentially promote, people from privileged demographic identity groups, especially blacks, women, LGBTQ+ individuals and, since 2021, people with disabilities. These policies have generated many charges that the IC is hiring less qualified people over heterosexual, healthy men of European origin. This section examines hiring policies and data and then addresses the critiques. This assessment is aided markedly by the publication of annual demographic data for the IC, a practice that DNI Clapper began in 2016 as a way to pressure his successors to continue preferential DEI hiring and promotion practices. But presumably not as Clapper intended, these publications also illustrate the ideological motives and desired results of DEI policies.

GAO benchmarks

The IC uses the two GAO benchmarks—comparable civilian work force and federal government employment data—to assess the political acceptability of its demographic statistics unless other comparisons seem more useful to rationalize DEI preferences.[141] The use of government- and economy-wide statistical standards applicable to all identity groups are used for comparison across all federal agencies, making clear that the

---

[139] National Alliance, "Report."
[140] Miranda Devine, "DEI hires pushed onto the FBI are putting the country's safety at risk for the sake of being 'woke," *New York Post*, January 24, 2024, https://nypost.com/2024/01/24/news/dei-hires-are-making-the-fbi-more-woke-than-qualified/.
[141] ODNI, Annual Demographic Report, Fiscal Year 2022, 6.

performance of groups or individuals, defined in any way, is not a concern. Because more demographic "diversity" is always better, intellectual diversity is irrelevant, and favored groups all have significant claims on DEI, there is no standard of comparison when numbers for one identity group are better, or improve more, than those of other groups. Using this box-checking logic, a near-ideal IC workforce might consist entirely of black, handicapped, Spanish-surnamed lesbians. Such an intersectionally uniform workforce would be completely "diverse," if for no other reason than that it could not be expanded further.

CIA director John Brennan promulgated in 2013 all of the recommendations of a panel formed by his predecessor, David Petraeus (2011-2012), and headed by former Secretary of State Madeleine Albright, to hire more women.[142] The goal was explicitly political, not performance-based. The number of women working at the CIA, their share of senior positions, and promotion rates were judged politically unacceptable, despite the fact that the study found no discrimination against women and attributed the gender imbalance in numbers to women's choices, including their decisions to quit agency work more frequently than men and to work part-time more often than men.[143] Women also acquired mentors less frequently than men. There has never been recognition of, let alone reflection upon, the fact that Department of Labor statistics show that men and women self-select into various career fields at sharply different rates.[144] For example, women are weakly represented among plumbers but substantially overrepresented among elementary school teachers. No matter. The once accurate but now groundless notion that women are discriminated against by our intelligence agencies remains politically and, evidently, emotionally attractive to some people, even though under Haspel women dominated the CIA's senior leadership.[145] It surely is also

---

[142] CIA, "Director's Advisory Group on Women in Leadership, Unclassified Report," March 2013, https://www.cia.gov/static/825c79d82205d8b8e0045a8dd87fc614/CIA _Women_In_Leadership_March2013.pdf.
[143] Ibid.
[144] U.S. Department of Labor, Employment and Earnings by Occupation, 2019, https://www.dol.gov/agencies/wb/data/occupations.
[145] For example, Liza Mundy, *The Sisterhood: The Secret History of Women at the CIA* (New York: Crown, 2023).

professionally advantageous for some women, who may be content to rely on DEI-based gender preferences to advance in their careers.

The U.S. government for years has sought to hire more black people despite the fact that the federal government as a whole employs far more blacks than OPM benchmarks—another reflection of favored minority status. The IC has followed suit. In the Obama years, the effort accelerated, but the intelligence agencies found it hard to increase numbers of black recruits for two reasons identified by CIA recruiters: (1) the pool of candidates who can meet tough IC hiring standards (educational attainment, lack of criminal record, drug-free status, etc.) is relatively small; and (2) competition to hire capable and qualified blacks is intense throughout the economy.[146] There long has been "systemic racism" in that government and private sector employers from the early days of "affirmative action" in the 1960s have eagerly hired even moderately capable black applicants over similarly qualified whites. The IC therefore often cannot compete with other organizations on the basis of status or salary. As a result, according to a former CIA recruiter, the recruiters often lied about the number of blacks they recruited because it was in their career interests to appear to meet quotas even if it meant misrepresenting the job descriptions of recruits once hired.[147] The recruiter revealed that blacks at IC agencies disproportionately occupy support positions—evidently a reflection of their lower collective skill levels that managers knew but could not overtly recognize. A common ruse was to report that blacks in support positions were line intelligence officers—a fib that must have had collaborators in management given the sensitivity of the issue and ease of checking the accuracy of such claims. In this and other ways noted in this book, CIA managers have likely generated ideology-motivated internal misinformation that hinders effective decision making. This occurred even as the CIA received and evidently continues to receive large numbers of high-quality applicants from other demographic groups.[148] While the CIA normally does not release such data publicly, former DCIA Michael Hayden said the CIA received 160,000 job applications in 2008; they

---

[146] Personal communications, various times.
[147] Personal communication, 2022.
[148] CIA public affairs officers, 2019 briefing to former CIA employees.

reportedly declined somewhat thereafter.[149] CIA public affairs officers told a large group of CIA alumni in 2019 that the agency then continued to receive large numbers of applications from high-quality people.

The IC CAE program

The GAO rarely investigates IC agencies or programs, but in 2019 it investigated one diversity-focused program, the IC Centers of Academic Excellence (IC CAE) program, finding it seriously deficient in important respects.[150] The program, which Congress created in 2005 and which the DIA administered from 2011 until it transitioned to the ODNI in fiscal year 2020, provided some $69 million in 46 grants through fiscal year 2021 to 29 colleges and universities with many minority students, especially historically black colleges and universities (HBCU) and schools with large Hispanic student bodies.[151] The IC CAE's stated purpose is to develop intelligence-related undergraduate courses that could increase the pool of "culturally and ethnically diverse" job applicants available to the IC, and thus recruit more ethnic minorities and people from rural areas.[152] Improving the performance of the IC is not one of the program's formally stated goals, although a frequent claim is that the "diversity" promoted by IC CAE enhances the IC's performance. Nevertheless, most IC CAE schools are not widely regarded as prestigious institutions, with Duke University standing as a rare exception. As in broader government diversity programs, moreover, IC CAE focuses on *domestic* demographic diversity and does little or nothing to recruit for diversity of outlook,

---

[149] Greg Myre, "CIA recruiting: The Rare Topic The Agency Likes To Talk About," NPR, March 26, 2018, https://www.npr.org/sections/parallels/2018/03/26/594909193/cia-recruiting-the-rare-topic-the-spy-agency-likes-to-talk-about.

[150] The program has a fairly detailed website, https://www.dia.mil/Training/IC-Centers-for-Academic-Excellence/Become-an-IC-CAE/.

[151] U.S. Government Accountability Office, *Intelligence Community: Actions Needed to Improve Planning and Oversight of the Centers for Academic Excellence Program*, GAO-19-529, Washington, DC, August 2019, 43-48.

[152] IC-CAE website, http://www.dia.mil/Training/IC-Centers-for-Academic-Excellence/. See also ODNI "Demographic Report: Hiring and Retention of Minorities, Women, and Persons with Disabilities in the United States Intelligence Community Fiscal Year 2016," 29-31; ODNI website, https://www.dni.gov/files/CHCO/documents/CAE/ICCAE_FAQs.pdf.

empathy, and expertise to address *foreign* intelligence challenges. Blacks, Hispanics, American Indians, women, LGBTQ+ individuals, and persons with disabilities do not inherently speak Arabic or understand Russian domestic politics or know North Korean nuclear weapons programs better than do healthy, heterosexual white males.

Perhaps unsurprisingly, the GAO found that the DIA's management of the IC CAE program was seriously deficient and that no measures of effectiveness or return on investment had even been designed, let alone measured accurately.[153] An academic study of IC CAE published in 2020 did not discuss performance in any meaningful way.[154] The GAO reported that the CIA, after initially working closely with 16 IC CAE schools, in 2014 reduced its involvement with the program, dealing with only six major universities.[155] The National Security Agency never dealt with any IC CAE institution, preferring to hire capable people from universities with good cybersecurity programs.[156]

A former CIA officer who does not want to be identified for fear of being called a racist confirmed, consistent with the GAO's cryptic observation, that the CIA's experience with IC CAE has not been favorable.[157] According to the officer, CIA personnel who visited HBCU schools were disappointed with their visits, and recruits from these schools experienced greater than average performance problems at the CIA. Another former intelligence officer, who had considerable experience working with IC CAE member schools, said some HBCUs merely added the word "intelligence" to the titles of already existing courses; in some cases, no one administering the program at participating colleges had a background in either education or intelligence.[158] The officer also reported that most IC agencies' recruits from HBCUs took support, not line

---

[153] U.S. GAO, *Intelligence Community: Actions Needed to Improve Planning and Oversight of the Centers for Academic Excellence Program*, 1.
[154] Michael Landon-Murray and Stephen Coulthart, "Intelligence Studies Programs as US Public Policy: A Survey of IC CAE Grant Recipients," *Intelligence and National Security* 35:2 (2020): 269-282.
[155] U.S. GAO, *Intelligence Community: Actions Needed to Improve Planning and Oversight of the Centers for Academic Excellence Program*, 31-32.
[156] Ibid., 12.
[157] Personal communication, 2019.
[158] Personal communication, 2020.

operational, jobs. A third intelligence officer, who administers online intelligence-related courses for a prominent university, confirmed that most black graduates of his university's intelligence program who work for the IC also hold support positions.[159] While support personnel such as security guards, human resources specialists, and logisticians fill important functions, they are not practicing intelligence officers, meaning that whatever "unique perspectives" they may have impart little or nothing to actual intelligence work.

On May 12-14, 2021, the IC CAE sponsored an online conference entitled "Workshop on Teaching Intelligence," which featured several prominent intelligence studies scholars and teachers. At the conference's conclusion, IC CAE director Michael Bennett made summary comments and asked attendees to send to him evidence that IC CAE had improved the performance of the IC. He said he was personally confident that it had, but he needed evidence to help justify IC CAE.[160] In essence, Bennett confirmed the GAO's conclusions of two years earlier: no hard data demonstrated IC CAE's effectiveness in achieving any of its stated goals, let alone in improving the IC's operational performance. The argument that diversity for its own sake is an unquestionable "good" reflecting "our values" continued to be its primary rationale for existence. Bennett's successor, Andrew ("Swede") Borene, admitted essentially the same point at an in-person conference in the autumn of 2022: there was no evidence that IC CAE improves the IC's performance.[161] A currently serving intelligence officer reported in 2024 that the ODNI still could not confirm that IC CAE improves the performance of U.S. intelligence but hoped to be able to do so within five years,[162] that is, after IC CAE will have been in existence for a quarter century or so.

DCIA Burns regularly extols the agency's efforts to hire more women and minorities.[163] He continues the hiring and promotion preferences

---

[159] Personal conversation, 2023.

[160] See conference recording.

[161] Source: a person who heard him speak.

[162] Personal communication, 2024.

[163] William Burns, *CIA Diversity, Equity, Inclusion and Accessibility Strategy, 2024-2025*, n.d., file:///C:/Users/Owner/Documents/John/Articles/Diversity%20dysfunction/articles/CIA_DEIA-Strategy_2024.pdf.

Brennan implemented in 2013—raising CIA's DEIA-juiced numbers further above OPM's benchmark figures.[164] Women in 2024 comprise slightly over half of CIA's employees, far more than women's share of the federal or national workforces. Burns has repeatedly expressed satisfaction with CIA progress in strengthening the Obama-era cultural changes that contributed to the outburst of political activism within the IC against Trump from 2016.

Disabilities valued

In the Biden years, the IC has, like the rest of the federal government, made a strong effort to hire persons with disabilities, now claiming incongruously that "disabled" people also improve operational performance. DIA for many years hired veterans with significant war wounds as part of its perceived obligation to disabled servicemen, but before the rise of DEI ideology did not claim they improved DIA's operational performance. This discussion has an Orwellian aspect. In the new logic, these people are assets not because they are veterans but because they are "differently abled,"[165] a category that is not limited to veterans. But people provided "accessibility" assistance really are handicapped or disabled. Dictionaries long have defined these terms as denoting a diminution of abilities of some sort. People get special pension benefits because they are disabled. Despite claims that disabled people are wonderful because they bring alternative "perspectives," or in the case of "neurodiverse" people, literally think differently in physiological terms, it seems certain that these people do not perform as well as healthy persons at most intelligence tasks or require significant help or accommodation, reducing their cost-effectiveness. People who question the IC's logic sometimes are now criticized for displaying the new ideological offense of "ableism," a transgression akin to "racism" or "sexism." This Orwellian Newspeak does not seem to trouble the IC's leaders. It is useful for diversity officers.

---

[164] Ibid.

[165] CIA, "Diversity and Inclusion Strategy, 2020-2023," March 2020, https://www.cia.gov/library/reports/DI_Strategy_2020.pdf, 5.

Increased public attention to "neurodiversity" makes the point that in a few areas of work—particularly in tasks associated with the computer industry—autistic people can perform well. But autistic workers reportedly perform well in relatively few job categories, typically require special handling by managers, and do not always fit effectively into standard workplace environments.[166] The IC does not talk about these limitations, for they are not ideologically useful.

Resource allocations

Diversity offices and programs consume considerable resources in many ways. The ODNI and the individual agencies do not publish many budget numbers or costs of specific activities. But the ODNI does publish a "top line" spending figure for the IC as a whole, which was $99.6 billion in fiscal year 2023.[167] We can, however, use other information sources to identify types and rough levels of efforts to enhance DEI-related political goals. These impose what economists call opportunity costs—in this case, the loss of intelligence activities that were not conducted because agency spending and other resources, such as employees' time, were instead dedicated to DEI programs.

The first and most obvious opportunity costs are the diversity officers themselves. While these individuals perform human resources (HR) functions, they are not part of HR departments per se. Hence, there is some duplication of effort. Each agency has at least one diversity office. The ODNI has two; as noted, one monitors the DEIA activities of the IC as a whole. The other administers DEIA policies within the ODNI only. The CIA has a main diversity office and one in each of its five directorates; some information suggests DCIA Haspel extended diversity offices one level lower—that is, to "offices" in the Directorate of Analysis, for example, which vary in number depending on periodic reorganizations but normally number around ten. State appears to have one diversity office for

---

[166] Preetika Rana, "Jobs Grow For Autistic Employees Beyond Tech Firms," *Wall Street Journal*, June 10, 2024, A1.

[167] ODNI, "U.S. Intelligence Community Budget," https://www.dni.gov/index.php/what-we-do/ic-budget.

each of its bureaus, including INR, an organization of about 450 people,[168] in addition to its main Office of Diversity and Inclusion created in 2021. These offices file many reports with at least the three executive branch offices noted above and interact with ODNI, departmental, and perhaps other government diversity offices or regulatory agencies.

Chief diversity officers and their principal staffers are senior officials, meaning they are well paid. Zakiya Carr Johnson, the State Department's current diversity and inclusion chief, is reportedly paid $180,000 per year,[169] nearly three times the average American salary in 2024. It is unknown exactly how many people in the IC focus exclusively on diversity issues, but many universities report spending tens of millions of dollars annually on DEI programs and staff. The University of Virginia, for example, which in recent years has had about 26,000 students, fewer than the IC has staff employees and contractors, reportedly spends about $20 million annually on salaries for 235 diversity staffers.[170]

The "A," for "Accessibility," in Biden's DEIA acronym, entails significant costs to provide facilities for the disabled. These include sign reader/translators for deaf people, specialized information technology systems for the blind, ramps and elevators for the physically disabled, and undoubtedly other varieties of support. The IC in Biden's years has substantially increased the number of people who are variously disabled. The IC's demographic report for fiscal year 2022 indicated that 8.7% of employees and 13.2% applicants were "persons with disabilities."[171] These numbers have risen sharply in recent years to figures far higher than those of the national labor force but below federal benchmarks. The

---

[168] Bureau of Intelligence and Research Fact Sheet, February 23, 2023, https://www. state.gov/inrfact-sheet/#:~:text=451%20Employees%2069%25%20Civil%20service %2016%25%20Foreign,service%2015%25%20Other%20Employees%20%28contra ctors%2C%20detailees%2C%20interns%29.

[169] Dave Seminara, "That Which Does Not Cull Us: Is Diversity Really 'Critical' to National Security?," *City Journal*, April 29, 2024.

[170] For example, James Bacon, "University of Virginia Spends $20 million on 235 DEI Employees, With Some Making $587,340 per Year," *The Jefferson Council*, March 5, 2024, https://thejeffersoncouncil.com/university-of-virginia-spends-20-million-on-235-dei-employees-with-some-making-587340-per-year/.

[171] ODNI, *Annual Demographic Report*, Fiscal Year 2022, 15, 18, file:///C:/Users/Owner/Documents/John/Articles/Diversity%20dysfunction/articles/O DNI_FY22_IC_Annual_Demographic_Report.pdf.

statistical reports identify two categories of disabled people: persons with disabilities (PWD), who were 7.2% of the IC workforce in fiscal year 2022, and the more seriously affected "persons with targeted disabilities" (PWTD), who comprised 1.6% of the IC workforce in the same period. The PWTD category seems most likely to describe people who require "accessibility" assistance.

The Dive issue noted above features an article by a deaf officer temporarily assigned abroad who required two sign interpreters. The foreign posting thus acquired one intelligence officer for the price of three professionals. We do not know the degree of severity of handicaps in the IC as a whole, but accommodations like the one described in the *Dive* suggest appreciable costs to help ensure "accessibility."

Training requirements impose time-related opportunity costs in addition to the financial costs of producing and administering the training programs, many of which are outsourced to external "diversity consultants" or similar contractors. "Diversity consultants," whose credentials often amount to little more than cursory certification courses administered by loosely regulated professional associations (and sometimes not even that), can charge thousands of dollars per hour for their services. They and their firms also bill substantial fees for training materials, which are generally undisclosed and have only sporadically become available thanks to whistleblowers, Freedom of Information Act (FOIA) requests, litigation discovery, deliberate violations of confidentiality requirements, or other irregular means that can involve significant personal risk to those revealing them. The explanation for this secrecy is readily apparent. Once divulged, diversity training materials in routine use across American institutions often turn out to be heavily biased against whites and males. In some cases, particularly involving universities, courts have found them to be unlawfully discriminatory. Nevertheless, DNI Clapper required all IC managers to take "unconscious bias" training, which is usually provided by contractors and appears to assign prejudicial sentiments to whites and males. In ICD 125, DNI Haines required all IC personnel to take an annual course on transgender sensitivities. The time spent on such courses is not used "productively." As noted, the IC CAE program spends several million dollars per year without generating any apparent performance enhancement, a result that the IC appears to accept since the program's main focus is obviously domestic politics.

The government sponsors associations of privileged demographic groups, such as the National Security Executives and Professionals Association mentioned above, pays for meetings such as periodic BIG conferences, provides travel funds for government employees to attend such meetings, and gives employees paid time off time to attend them.[172] These costs seem to have risen substantially in the Obama years, evidently remain high, and will almost certainly increase if IC priorities remain as they are. One recent international assessment of the global DEI industry estimates its 2023 value at $10.9 billion, projected to rise to $24.4 billion by 2030.[173]

The Marxist purpose of diversity policies is to create and enhance divisions between groups of people—the deceptive platitudes of Marxists and people who naively believe their slogans notwithstanding. DEI has successfully created social conflicts, sometimes expressed in formal grievances, which need to be adjudicated, adding more layers of costs. Managers handle some grievances informally, but diversity offices duplicate the functions of both human resources departments and inspectors general, handling other complaints formally in investigative processes that often go on for months and occupy the time and energy not only of investigators, but administrative personnel, complainants, witnesses, and respondents, who are in many cases removed from work and placed on leave pending resolution. As DEI becomes more controversial, contested investigations increasingly go to court, costing the agencies, the Justice Department, and, ultimately, the taxpayer yet more funds to litigate and, if necessary, settle or pay judgments in them. Some

---

[172] Numerous personal communications.

[173] http://www.researchandmarkets.com/reports/5519706/diversity-and-inclusion-dandi-global-strategic?utm_source=CI&utm_medium=PressRelease&utm_code=z 2ql4x&utm_campaign=1941357+-+Global+Diversity+and+Inclusion+(D%26I)+ Strategic+Research+Report+2024%3a+Market+to+Reach+%2424.4+Billion+by+20 30++Top+Diversity%2c+Equity%2c+and+Inclusion+Trends+for+2023+and+Beyon d&utm_exec=chdomspi.

lawyers now specialize in intelligence law,[174] just as others specialize in litigation involving corporate or educational DEI investigations. DEI has been a boon to such lawyers. Some examples of DEI-motivated litigation are presented below.

In addition to the costs described above, there are also celebrations of the various special interests of the DEIA confederation, most of which are a month long in the federal government. In June 2024, in celebration of Pride Month, the ODNI invited all IC personnel to come during work hours to get their nails painted in rainbow colors or learn how to crochet a Pride flag—all on government time and at government expense.[175]

The categories listed herein suggest that DEIA spending may amount to as much as a few percentage points of the IC's total budget. If the many varieties of diversity-related costs are only two percent of total IC spending, spending on DEIA programs at the current level would be in the range of $2 billion per year—a sum that could otherwise buy a lot of intelligence collection, analysis, and field operations. The full opportunity costs are unknowable.

Diversity officers' activism

Diversity offices and diversity-related polices affect the day-to-day conduct of intelligence activities in many ways in addition to their significant resource costs. As more diversity offices sprout across the IC, their activism and effects are also growing.

Fred Fleitz, a former CIA analyst and member of the House intelligence committee staff, argued in 2016 that DCIA Brennan's diversity strategy was misguided and destructive in practice.[176] Noting that Brennan claimed that increasing demographic diversity improved the

---

[174] For a discussion of this topic by a prominent intelligence attorney, Mark Zaid, see interview of him on a "Spycast" podcast, at https://thecyberwire.com/podcasts/spycast/625/transcript.

[175] Elizabeth Lawrence, "Biden intel agencies celebrating 'Pride Month' with 'transgender' flag manicures and more," American Military News, June 18, 2024, https://americanmilitarynews.com/2024/06/biden-intel-agencies-celebrating-pride-month-with-transgender-flag-manicures-and-more/.

[176] Fred Fleitz, "The Obama CIA Is Putting Diversity above National Security," National Review, February 23, 2016, https://www.nationalreview.com/2016/02/cia-diversity-strategy-misguided-dangerous/.

CIA's ability to accomplish its missions, Fleitz argued that Brennan had instead created "diversity quotas" for hiring and promotion that deemphasized "competence and achievement:"

> Brennan has mandated "diversity and inclusion performance objectives for all CIA managers and supervisors and ultimately the entire workforce," so that CIA personnel must weigh diversity and gender figures in making key assignments and senior-level promotions. Brennan's plan also includes agency-wide "unconscious bias" training.[177]

As Fleitz argued, Brennan advanced President Obama's agenda at the expense of national security. "The CIA's mission is too serious to be distracted by Obama's social-engineering efforts,"[178] he wrote, adding:

> It is not unjust to hire a white male with a Ph.D. from Harvard and a background in nuclear science to analyze the Iranian nuclear program over someone with weaker credentials who is a member of a racial or gender minority. Altering the rules so the latter candidate will win a competition for such a job is not in our national interest. Adding such considerations to CIA promotion rules will further complicate the agency's management, which is already suffering from politicization and political correctness. This is why in the CIA Directorate of Intelligence, where I worked for 19 years, many highly qualified officers refuse to apply for management jobs — or they last in them for only a few years before returning to analyst positions.[179]

Scott C. Uehlinger, who retired as a CIA operations officer in 2014, wrote in 2017 from a slightly different perspective:

> The twin serpents of politicization and political correctness—a Soviet term, by the way—walk hand in hand throughout the intelligence community, as well as every other government agency. The PC mindset that now dominates every college

---

[177] Ibid.
[178] Ibid.
[179] Ibid.

campus is also positioned firmly throughout our government—particularly within the intelligence community, which saw its greatest personnel influx ever in the post-9/11 environment. Today's intelligence community, the average age of which I would estimate at 32, was raised under the beleaguered Bush administration and reached professional maturity primarily under the Obama administration, immersed in a PC environment. [180]

A CIA officer recounted in 2023 one way in which CIA diversity offices affect operations—consistent with, but beyond, those noted by Fleitz and Uehlinger.[181] According to this officer, it has become common for employees of favored demographic identity groups to complain to a diversity office if they receive criticism from managers about their daily work or in their annual performance appraisals. Reportedly, diversity officials frequently side with complainers, levying punishments on managers who, in this source's view, generally do traditional managerial duties—including overseeing, rating, and trying to improve employees' performance—well. As a result, good managers have been inappropriately punished, leading other managers who observe this pattern to refrain from criticizing, and even to reward, shoddy performance in order to avoid the wrath of diversity officers. In this way, the diversity offices operate in ways roughly consistent with the political commissars who oversaw the Soviet Red Army and Chinese Communist Party officials who now "supervise" many Chinese institutions. Like them, diversity "commissars" can overrule line managers when ideological orthodoxy is threatened. Hence, the quality of management is damaged, and the quality of work is diminished.

Fleitz, Uehlinger, and the CIA officer cited above all raise an important issue we can flag but not quantify. Leadership is important. Leaders help units perform better in many ways, but largely because they inspire better performance from their subordinates. If good natural leaders

---

[180] Scott C. Uehlinger, "How the intel community was turned into a political weapon against President Trump," *The Hill*, April 5, 2017, http://thehill.com/blogs/pundits-blog/the-administration/327413-how-the-intel-community-was-turned-into-a-political.

[181] Personal communication, 2023.

are opting to avoid formal leadership positions because they perceive DEI policies to be malevolently intolerant or immoral, or because they do not wish to become vulnerable to unwarranted complaints, collective performance will decline. This seems to be happening, although the magnitude of this problem is unclear and the consequences may well lie in the future.

The anecdotal evidence is supported from a different perspective by Barry Zulauf, who was then the Intelligence Community Analytic Ombudsman, a senior ODNI position. Zulauf observed in October 2020:

> I have seen in the comments brought to my attention as Analytic Ombudsman where analysts confuse editing or constructive criticism as politicization. I am afraid we have a whole generation now in the workforce who have never had a harsh word spoken to them or never had any criticism expressed to them in college as they express their "feelings" on issues. Such snowflake treatment does not prepare them well for the kind of give-and-take needed to make for rigorous analysis.[182]

But then, one of main purposes of DEI is to provide "snowflake treatment" to privileged identity groups, continuing the "snowflake treatment" many students now receive as a matter of policy at many American universities.[183] As Zulauf rightly noted, it was precisely the rigorous, and sometimes tough, conversations of the review process that improved agencies' corporate analytic products by trying to eradicate biases of all sorts. This process cannot work if ideology trumps competence and employees are granted "safe spaces" for their "feelings" or "lived experiences" at the expense of intellectual rigor, and if management imposes DEI-related ideological orthodoxy on intelligence analyses.

Such an activist approach is no longer limited to the CIA and ODNI. As noted, numerous FBI personnel have reported similar problems at their agency in the Biden years.[184] An employee of the NSA recounted in 2023

---

[182] Zulauf email to author, October 11, 2020.
[183] For example, Greg Lukianoff and Jonathan Haidt, *The Coddling of the American Mind: How Good Intentions and Bad Ideas Are Setting Up a Generation for Failure* (New York: Penguin, 2018); Mac Donald, *The Diversity Delusion*.
[184] National Alliance, "Report," 54-61.

that an NSA person wrote an unclassified story for one of that agency's internal publications that contained a reference to a person with a mobility problem. The diversity office insisted on appreciable revisions to language in the draft article and delayed its publication for several months.[185] This episode was operationally inconsequential, but raised in the mind of the person who reported the episode the important question: just what does the diversity office do and what are its larger implications?

While we cannot directly tie other dysfunctions of the IC workforce causally to DEI policies, ongoing social change and the politicization of students of all ages suggest strong linkages. The characteristics noted below seem likely to have facilitated to some extent acceptance of DEI policies by many employees, and been reinforced by them. Scholars with intelligence backgrounds have begun to write about such associations. For example, Margaret Marangione, a former CIA analyst, cited surveys indicating that 58 percent of college students scored higher on a narcissism test in 2009 than did students in 1982, and that Narcissistic Personality Disorder (NPD) diagnoses are nearly three times higher in millennials than in persons over 65.[186] CIA psychologist Ursula Wilder observed that the combination of entitlement and narcissism is strongly associated with leaking by intelligence personnel.[187] (DEI is, of course, all about giving various forms of entitlements to privileged groups.) Similarly, former CIA security officer Terence Thompson argued that narcissism and disgruntlement are abetted by three phenomena that have recently become more prominent in the intelligence workforce: "grandiose needs for recognition," a "culture of non-restraint," and anonymity—until leakers wish to become public figures.[188] All of these traits became more visible at the CIA in 2016 and later, when the observers above wrote, after the Obama-Clapper-Brennan resocialization processes were well along.

---

[185] Personal communication, 2023.

[186] Margaret S. Marangione, "Millennials: Truthtellers or Threats?" *International Journal of Intelligence and CounterIntelligence* 32:2 (2019): 356.

[187] Ursula M. Wilder, "The Psychology of Espionage and Leaking in the Digital Age," *Studies in Intelligence* 61:2 (Extracts, 2017): 24-27.

[188] Terence J. Thompson, "A Psycho-Social Motivational Theory of Mass Leaking," *International Journal of Intelligence and CounterIntelligence* 31:1 (2018): 116, 119.

Some observers point to more distant linkages, especially to long-term influence operations by the Soviet Union. Former Assistant Director of Central Intelligence for Administration James Simon pointed to the influence of activist groups and the disinformation programs of Russia and other countries as causes of some of the evolution in the IC's cultures.[189] Some FBI personnel agree.[190] Still other analysts have postulated broad social influences observable in the politicization of American universities, and thus indirectly of the IC, including the development of Marxist "critical theory"—the direct antecedent of DEI policies.[191] These thoughts surely have some bases in fact, but actual influence mechanisms and their effect remain unclear and may be modest or coincidental. The nature and consequences of links between these characteristics on the one hand, and acceptance of DEI and operational dysfunctions, is a complicated subject still demanding comprehensive research.

Managers' diversity-related policies

Leaders make decisions based on the guidance they receive from above—from senior managers and the diversity offices—including overt instructions and implicit incentives regarding DEI. They set specific policies for their organizations and establish credible incentives applicable to decisions about staffers' careers and operations. Some are wise, some are not. These include DEI-influenced promotion and assignment decisions. People who do what senior managers want get promoted, especially given that adherence to DEI goals is now a formal performance criterion upon which employees are judged at most, if not all, IC agencies.

---

[189] James Simon, email to author, June 20, 2020.
[190] National Alliance, "Report," 62.
[191] For example, see Thomas Rid, *Active Measures: The Secret History of Disinformation and Political Warfare* (New York: Farrar, Straus and Giroux, 2020); Ion Mihai Pacepa and Ronald J. Rychlak, *Disinformation* (Washington: WND, 2013); Mike Gonzales, *The Plot to Change America: How Identity Politics Is Dividing the Land of the Free* (New York: Encounter, 2020); John A. Gentry, "Belated Success: Soviet Active Measures against the United States," *American Intelligence Journal* 39:2 (2022): 151-170; J. Michael Waller, *Big Intel: How the CIA and FBI Went from Cold War Heroes to Deep State Villains* (Washington: Regnery, 2024); Mike Gonzales and Katharine Cornell Gorka, *Next Gen Marxism: What It Is and How to Combat It* (New York: Encounter, 2024).

At the CIA, annual performance assessments—the Performance Appraisal Reports (PARs, pronounced as a word)—list in at least general terms the standards of performance against which employees are graded and ranked against their peers in specific professional categories. PAR commentary and associated ratings of employees make or break careers. Such strong DEI-related incentives firmly embed leaders' ideological views in the organizational cultures of the CIA and all other DEI-influenced government agencies. The CIA reportedly requires its personnel to take diversity courses annually.[192] Successful (or not) completion of such courses reportedly is noted on PARs.[193]

To summarize findings thus far, we can list major DEI-related policies. We know institutional incentives are designed to encourage employees to accept DEI policies and act in accordance with them. We also know that managerial decisions and actions have operational consequences. Brennan, especially, and others have told employees to be politically active in support of DEI policies and more generally in support of the political agendas of the Obama and Biden administrations. We can track resource allocations that reflect such decisions in some cases. It therefore is unsurprising that employees frequently embed DEI orthodoxy in their operational activities, just as DCIA Burns and Secretary Blinken have desired. These factors intersect in various ways in the vignettes that follow.

Operational implications

DEI-related policies have had numerous immediate and indirect operational implications. We can divide these effects into several varieties. The first group damages the quality of the workforce and the ability of intelligence officers to work together collegially. This complex of factors affects the major CIA missions of collection and analysis. And, not insignificantly, the overt politicization of 2016-2021 generated by purposeful, DEI-motivated alterations of CIA's organizational culture in the Brennan years—and elsewhere in the Biden years—has rendered U.S.

---

[192] Personal communication, 2024.
[193] Numerous personal communications, 2023 and 2024.

intelligence suspect in the minds of many Americans, including government decisionmakers and citizens generally.

Damage to workforce competence and collegiality

A large body of reporting indicates that DEI logic and politics have led to the hiring and promotion of many people who are not as able as competitors from non-favored demographic groups, especially white males. Unfortunately, the agencies refuse to provide hard data useful for quantifying such claims and counterclaims, and their published demographic reports do little to address this issue.

Easier to document and assess are assertions that DEI policy and related managerial decisions and organizational cultural changes have balkanized the workforce and generated tensions and distrust—just as the Marxist designers of DEI intended. The heavy-handed orthodoxy of DEI is causing massive self-censorship by people across society who do not support the DEI agenda. Many Americans now self-censor for political reasons.[194] A now-retired senior CIA manager of analysts wrote while he was still working: "As the workforce has gotten larger, so has diversity. Political correctness rules. With the increased political divide, it is hard to be outspoken. We choose our close colleagues carefully."[195]

The immediate consequence of such divisions is that teamwork is damaged. Employees do not trust each other in the way they once did. A State Department official noted that employees are now divided in a new way—people who accept Biden's DEIA agenda including its Small Steps program and those who do not.[196] People "look over their shoulders" and worry about perceptions of "compliance with ideological dictates."[197] An analyst at a major IC agency described himself as a "coward" for not speaking out against DEI and the related rise of Marxist influences in

---

[194] James L. Gibson and Joseph L. Sutherland, "Keeping Your Mouth Shut: Spiraling Self-Censorship in the United States," *Political Science Quarterly* 138:3 (2023): 361–376.
[195] Personal communication, 2021.
[196] Personal communication, 2022.
[197] Personal communication, 2022.

academic intelligence studies.[198] He is in fact a very decent person who has shown great courage in assessing intelligence organizations on many topics, but as a mid-career professional with a family he considers it wise to be carefully self-protective concerning DEI. Still others say quietly that they oppose the prominent support for LGBTQ+ issues on moral or theological grounds but do not speak out; they, too, are wise to hide their beliefs in environments of intolerant ideological orthodoxy.[199]

According to a retired senior female CIA operations officer, preferential treatment for women is controversial and divisive within the CIA. While some women favor it, men feel discriminated against[200] and many senior women who succeeded in traditional ways, such as the officer in question, feel their legitimate accomplishments and reputations are diminished.[201] There are chronic hints, she said, that people wonder whether senior female officers actually earned their promotions, as opposed to receiving them on DEI grounds. There is no way such suspicions can be definitively confirmed or refuted.

Similarly, a retired senior manager of analysts who retains close ties to many CIA officers reported that white men feel institutionally discriminated against. He estimated in 2019 that human resources office staffs were about 80% female.[202] Indeed, at most IC organizations, and elsewhere, diversity and personnel offices are staffed overwhelmingly by women and minorities, many of whom are candid about their personal gender- and race-oriented political agendas. By comparison, a 2024 study of the "top" fifty American universities ranked by *U.S. News and World Report* found that 80% of those schools' chief diversity officers are black despite blacks only comprising about 13% of the U.S. population. A mere two percent are white. The study concluded that universities' "chief diversity officers are not very diverse," a judgment that seems to apply to

---

[198] Personal communication, 2023. For a description of Marxist "critical intelligence studies," see Gentry, "Ideology in Costume."
[199] Multiple personal communications over several years.
[200] For a description of this situation more broadly, see Jeremy Carl, *The Unprotected Class: How Anti-White Racism Is Tearing America Apart* (New York: Regnery, 2024).
[201] Discussions with former senior CIA officers, 2019.
[202] Conversation with author, September 2019.

the U.S. government as well.[203] A common pejorative quip, given the shifting ideological tone of the federal workforce, is that federal employees collectively are still "too male, pale, and stale." (Sometimes, "Yale" is added to the snide remark). While this remark is on its face sexist, racist, and ageist, it is not considered a transgression, for only favored groups under the DEI system can legitimately complain about discriminatory comments.

Even former CIA operations officer Marc Polymeropoulos, who achieved considerable infamy for co-writing the open letter, signed by 51 former intelligence officers, that deceptively insinuated in October 2020 that the contents of Hunter Biden's abandoned laptop computer, which contained emails suggesting that he and his father had engaged in political corruption, was Russian disinformation, sees a problem. Polymeropoulos lamented in early 2024 that cultural changes in new operations officers generate work habit differences and "woke" political attitudes sufficiently different from long-time perspectives as to warrant "counseling."[204]

As a longtime, currently serving intelligence analyst at an agency other than the CIA summarized with understatement in 2024, "DEI policies have been a distraction from our core mission."[205] Another, senior officer at an agency other than the CIA assessed the operational implications of DEIA policies, concluding "it negatively affects our mission."[206]

DEI policies affect CIA operations and analysis negatively, but in different ways depending on who is affected. Anecdotes in the next section are lightly edited for clarity and to obscure the identity of their authors and relevant protagonists.

---

[203] Emily Fowler, "Most university chief diversity officers are black," *The College Fix*, July 25, 2024, https://www.thecollegefix.com/most-university-chief-diversity-officers-are-black/.

[204] Marc Polymeropoulos, "Gen Z and CIA is a Relationship in Need of Counseling," *Cipher Brief*, January 29, 2024, https://www.thecipherbrief.com/column_article/gen-z-and-cia-is-a-relationship-in-need-of-counseling.

[205] Personal communication.

[206] Personal communication, 2023.

Implications for Operations

Data regarding DEI influences on operations in the field are few, but those available illustrate implications of the policies noted above. As a former CIA case officer recounted DEI-influenced field policies and activities:

> A female minority was assigned as COS [Chief of Station]. She was an unfit leader and was allowed to "retire early" to save face while being removed early from this last field assignment. Her background ... she was one of two females previously put out in the field of her division as the division's first women COSes when diversity and inclusion initiatives were on a roll. She underperformed in that field assignment and regularly had her decisions countermanded by Headquarters (not rumor, she even admitted this to subordinates). She went from COS of an important station in her division to being sent back to Hqs for a singleton job in that division—literally no subordinates. Not sure what led her to then be sent to another large station in the field, in a different division, but diversity was blamed by all who knew her background (causing morale problems for all of us who had to sit under her obviously flawed leadership ability). She would have 3-hour-long staff meetings every day. You can imagine how that affected performance and morale. She broke down crying in two staff meetings that I was in. Division, after hearing the horror stories from many TDYers [temporary duty visitors], started sending senior management out to investigate (including the division chief and the deputy and the COPS [chief of operations]). It was miserable and also affected our relations with partners.[207]

A CIA case officer described how DEI issues affected operations in his/her first overseas assignment:

> The COB [Chief of Base] was a minority man who had flamed out at his previous post as a manager within a large station. (All accounts indicated that he was unfit for leadership and faced a rebellion of his entire staff.). He was removed from his previous

---

[207] Written communication to author.

post and decided to file a lawsuit, claiming he was being removed for reasons of racial discrimination. As the story goes, during the legal proceedings, an opposing lawyer made a note about him that used a term that could be construed as a racial slur. Discovery of that error caused the case to die and for him to be reinstated into a leadership role for a second chance in another division. That appointment—which occurred because of a diversity-related issue, even though he had a clear track record of nonperformance—created total chaos for the new base. He was so bad that officers literally agreed that, if he came to one of our houses after hours, we would not let him in. Officers put traps on their safes to see if he was going in at night and looking through their stuff. He was reading all of our emails, in and out. He once threatened me and another officer, "If I go down, you all go down." As a young, new DO [Directorate of Operations] officer, I would occasionally wait until late at night to get on a secure phone with trusted senior officers to seek guidance. Long story short, after a very painful time for all involved, multiple visits to the base by senior division managers (including the chief, the deputy, etc.) the division stepped in and removed him, then put him in a singleton job in a nearby field station. This deeply affected our relationship with partners (the Drug Enforcement Administration in particular, as this was a station heavily focused on counternarcotics).

A fairly senior former case officer reported this anecdote:

I was sitting on a panel doing annual performance appraisals of employees, [and] had to assess a young case officer who was both an ethnic minority and identified as LGBTQ. Her underperformance was very carefully and well documented. She was described by her station management as disruptive because she would charge discrimination anytime she was challenged about her performance. According to her rater, who was a station branch chief, she had been like this since her first day on the streets after case officer training and, whether it was true or not, she was regarded as a diversity hire who had made it through the training (and was now failing terribly) because the wrong criteria were used to move her through the system. She was very disruptive for morale, according to the manager. We could not promote her based on her track record of nonperformance. Her managers expected a legal challenge, but I do not know if that ever surfaced. I was reassigned to a field position again and lost touch with the situation.

In the Biden years, a male case officer in the middle of a good overseas tour, having multiple recruits to his credit, had spent months cultivating another potentially valuable asset.[208] When he told his chief of station that recruitment seemed imminent, the COS asked the man if he would transfer credit for the upcoming recruitment to a female case officer who had not thus far in her tour recruited anyone. The woman had no role in this recruitment effort. Disturbed, the case officer asked for advice from a more experienced case officer located elsewhere. When asked if the female case officer was a good person and a good case officer, the man replied, "She tries hard." After consideration, the man suggested to his COS that credit for the recruitment be shared evenly with the woman. The COS agreed. Three lessons from this episode are evident: (1) this COS, and implicitly the CIA given established incentives, sometimes values promotion of DEI over actual operational performance; (2) "trying hard" seems to be as valuable as performing well, reflecting damage to, if not abandonment of, former meritocratic standards; and (3) formally reported, bogus credits for performing a core DO mission misinforms senior CIA managers about the performance of their personnel, potentially seriously misleading them about the actual operational value of specific people and DEI policies in general. Probably no one knows how much of a problem this is. Internal survey research potentially could produce a rough estimate of the magnitude and salience of the problem.

An operations officer described life at headquarters:

I was in Headquarters [at Langley, Virginia] in a division that was between chiefs. The deputy, a white man, was the favored

---

[208] Source: a knowledgeable person.

candidate to move up. He was very competent and was well-liked by all. A contender, a minority female who had a track record of not being liked by subordinates because of her caustic personality, filed a lawsuit, charging discrimination when she was not selected. We went without a division chief for something like a half year as this all played out. Long story short, she was handed the job. (The division's weekly meeting included references to Elton John's "The Bitch is Back" when it became clear she had won.) Immediately, she began changing the leadership of the office according to diversity characteristics. Every key position was quickly filled by women or minorities until the makeup of the office no longer represented the U.S. population. As a measure of her toxicity, she regularly made subordinate managers cry. An example involved a low branch-level manager who was also a minority female and who was called into the chief's office to be accused of having ambitions to replace the chief, a particularly puzzling incident given the vast difference in rank and positions. Queen Bee complex was in full play. This deeply affected morale, as you can imagine.

A former CIA operations officer recounted:

In one station, we had a position for a single officer located about 1-2 hours away that required a seasoned operations officer who could operate on their own. We brought in a female case officer whose paperwork implied that she was the best candidate. We found out later that her home division had been passing her off to other divisions for years and kept her PARs [Performance Appraisal Reports] decent looking to prevent lawsuits (she was very litigious). We saw issues, and began documenting, within her first three months. She couldn't write cables at the level expected of someone at her grade, was not going out and making contacts (the bread and butter of the case officer), was submitting accounting for meetings with people of no operational value (social contacts), etc. So, in addition to careful documentation, I had to begin working with her to improve her performance, which took away from my other duties. She claimed to our Deputy Chief of Station (DCOS) that I was "harassing" her by trying to get her to do her job. Fortunately, our DCOS (a woman) saw through this nonsense, and we soon removed this officer from her position. She went back to Headquarters to finish out her days in the Operations Center (not exactly the golden last tour for a case officer). Anyway, here was a personnel decision (allowing an underperforming person to continue worming [her] way through the system because [she was] willing to pull the diversity card when held accountable and no one wanted to deal with that). I lost many productive hours—when I should have been working with first tour officers learning the trade—to try to make this person productive and then, finally, to gracefully facilitate an exit. The work she was hired to do was never done, so we lost all that potential productivity (intel, recruitments, etc.).[209]

Perhaps the most prominent potential implication of DEI policies involved the death of seven CIA personnel in a suicide bombing at Camp Chapman near Khost, Afghanistan, on December 30, 2009.[210] One of the deadliest incidents in CIA history, it was unsurprisingly much discussed internally and provoked significant public commentary. While the episode remains controversial, one relevant aspect of the tragedy here is that a member of the CIA's team at Khost, and one of the victims, was Jennifer Matthews, a career analyst. While Matthews was apparently considered to be a fine analyst, she was not an operations officer and had no operational paramilitary expertise, let alone command experience in a combat zone. She had just finished a four-year tour in Europe as a counterterrorism analyst when she went to Afghanistan.[211] She reportedly was a favorite of some senior managers. She was given the job, evidently because she wanted, and senior managers supported, her assignment to a coveted

---

[209] Personal communication, March 2023.
[210] Joby Warrick, *The Triple Agent: The al-Qaeda Mole Who Infiltrated the CIA* (New York: Doubleday, 2011).
[211] Ibid., 20.

combat command in order to enable her to be promoted into the Senior Intelligence Service.[212]

Matthews's friends recognized the danger, and at least one told her not to take the job. But she had plenty of self-confidence and wanted a promotion. Critics charge that she did not do enough to vet the individual who carried out the suicide bombing and let too many agency people get too close to him when he came to the base, increasing the bomb's toll. As a former CIA officer recounted:

> Regarding Khost, I worked in CTC [Counterterrorism Center] after that happened. There were many times when I encountered conversations from veteran CTC officers about Matthews's lack of qualifications for the job—a common quip being that she went from being a reports officer in Europe to a paramilitary base in a war zone in the Middle East. (At the same time, there was a strong effort by CTC management to quash any such talk). I never heard her assignment spoken of in terms of favoritism, but I suppose it was implied by the perpetuation of the idea that she simply wasn't qualified for the job (and her decisions led to the death of officers). Also, there was a very strong personality in the senior ranks at the time who went on to become the chief of the center who had a reputation for doling out assignments and promotions to favorites. This strong personality was often said to carry guilt for the Khost incident, but I don't know if that is because he assigned an unqualified officer or ultimately gave the go ahead on the meeting that ended in disaster.[213]

DEI affects operations in other parts of CIA as well. During the Brennan years in the Directorate of Support—the administrative support arm of CIA—a young black man was assigned to lead a relatively small unit working on logistics issues. According to a person with direct knowledge of the unit, he was inept to the point that he did literally no work.[214] Two white subordinates on their own initiative divided his duties

---

[212] Ibid., 24.
[213] Personal communication, 2023.
[214] Personal communication, 2023.

among themselves, meaning the unit as a whole performed adequately. The two white employees, however, each did half again more work than they were assigned, and paid, to do. They evidently did so without complaint. Despite widespread knowledge of his deficiencies, the inept manager received stellar performance appraisals and was promoted. FBI veterans report similar episodes of deteriorating recruitment standards and lower quality personnel due to DEI,[215] and recent scandals in academia suggest that certain minorities have attained employment and sometimes high-level promotions – including to the presidency of Harvard University – at least in part due to DEI considerations.[216]

These anecdotes illustrate an important point: many senior managers are well aware of the problems that DEI policies have created and continue to produce. They sometimes have taken or permitted some remedial actions, often very carefully and with political sensitivity. But at many other times managers knowingly let DEI-generated ineptitude prosper; the tried and true ethic of meritocracy has clearly been seriously damaged. The evidence presented herein contains no evidence that managers have addressed the root causes of such problems—evidently because DEI ideology is now so deeply embedded in the ranks of senior career officials of federal agencies, as well as in the political appointees who nominally lead them, that recognizing the reality of DEI-caused problems amounts to career suicide. Indeed, this author spoke in 2019 with a senior CIA officer who had authority to initiate an internal inquiry into the practical, operational implications of DEI policies. When I proposed such a project, he seemed horror-stricken. I thought in retrospect that I might as well have asked him to jump off the top of a tall building or in front of a speeding train. He unsurprisingly did not conduct such a study. It would have been career suicide even for a senior official.

Implications for analysis

DEI-related managerial problems of the sort afflicting CIA operations also affect the analysis directorate, and did so even in the era of "affirmative

---

[215] National Alliance, "Report," 67-70, 80-96.
[216] Paul du Quenoy, "Lessons from the removal of Harvard's president," *Spectator*, January 3, 2024.

action." A former CIA officer recounted an experience in the analysis directorate in the 1990s as a newly hired officer:

> My office was all Caucasian, except for a few Asians. We took on a young new hire who was black. The boss, a white woman, literally told me that he was a diversity hire (for her, in our office) and that he would improve our chances in the annual office picnic football game. He did not do well and ended up leaving after a few years (left the Agency all together to go into business). He was very personable, and well liked. His reason for being in the office was not a secret (I don't know if anyone ever pulled him aside and discussed it with him), and I have to believe it affected the way he was treated and, very possibly, his ability to perform. (Granted, there are many performance-related issues and other things that could cause someone to not do well and to ultimately leave, but I am inclined to include the decision to hire him as a diversity hire as one variable in the outcome).[217]

Even before the increased emphasis on hiring blacks, a retired CIA analyst recounted that in the mid-1980s the unit of the analysis directorate (then called the Directorate of Intelligence) that published the *President's Daily Brief* (*PDB*) employed a young black man as a quality control analyst.[218] His job was to check the facts of draft submissions for consideration for publication in the *PDB* (and also the other current intelligence product of the day, the *National Intelligence Daily*). According to the analyst, the black officer was widely seen as incompetent. He reportedly regularly missed errors in drafts and also frequently changed accurate statements to inaccurate ones. One staffer said he thought the individual, a graduate of an HBCU, read at about a fourth-grade level. Managers clearly recognized that they had a problem but also knew they could not just transfer the individual, so they gave him extra training, without much effect, and had other staff check his work, imposing an opportunity cost problem. Managers found that despite their extra vigilance some of his minor errors made their way into final *PDB*

---

[217] Source email to author, 2023.
[218] Personal communication, 2024.

"books" that went to the Reagan White House. The individual evidently rotated to another job at the end of "normal" tour on the *PDB* staff. This case is especially notable because affirmative action damaged the quality of analyses going directly to the president. As in other cases, especially in later years, managers knew they had a problem but for political reasons had to address it in a very different, suboptimal (from the performance perspective) way than if the employee had been white.

More importantly, it is well established in the intelligence literature that biases of all sorts generate closed minds and analytic errors. Such biases sometimes generate major intelligence failures. For example, Luke Benjamin Wells has shown how British and American intelligence officers, working from virtually identical raw data, reached very different conclusions in the 1950s about the size and purpose of Soviet strategic bombing forces based in their collective assumptions about Soviet intentions concerning Britain and the USA, respectively, and bureaucratic interests.[219] Former chairman of the National Intelligence Council John Gannon (1997-2001) has recounted how he was sometimes frustrated by the close-mindedness of analytic offices in the IC and asked his national intelligence officer for warning, Robert Vickers (1996-2004), to both prod line units and provide alternative analyses.[220] Former CIA officer Richards Heuer has documented the importance of cognitive biases in analysis by both individuals and groups and offered ways to minimize them.[221] Heuer mentioned "motivated biases" like DEI only in passing, presumably because when he wrote in the 1990s and before he knew that the agency's quality control mechanism in the form of "review processes" then successfully excised most such biases.[222]

But times change and things do not always improve. Important biases in analysis appeared in the Obama years. As noted, Michael Hayden wrote that the failure to warn of Russian meddling in the 2016 U.S. presidential

---

[219] Luke Benjamin Wells, "The 'bomber gap': British intelligence and an American delusion," *Journal of Strategic Studies* 40:7 (2017): 963-989.

[220] John A. Gentry and Joseph S. Gordon, *Strategic Warning Intelligence: History, Challenges, and Prospects* (Washington: Georgetown University Press, 2019), 83.

[221] Richards J. Heuer, Jr., *Psychology of Intelligence Analysis* (Washington DC: Center for the Study of Intelligence, 1999).

[222] Gentry, "Managers of Analysts."

election stemmed from line analysts' biased effort to help make Obama's "reset" policy regarding Russia work—a variety of purposeful bias in analysis that the review process is designed to prevent.[223] While the CIA history staff has been very good about recounting analytic successes and failures of the distant past, nothing in the public sphere addresses the implications for analysis of DEI policies or the organizational cultural changes they have wrought. It seems to be a taboo subject.

Hence, we have few publicly detailed accounts of how Obama-era politicization influenced actual IC analyses. David G. Muller Jr., a retired naval intelligence officer who worked at the National Counterterrorism Center (NCTC) in 2009-2014, has provided a useful case study of how President Obama's views of Islam—a DEI focus still—altered the way the IC in general viewed, and may continue to view, Islamist terrorism and demographic diversity in the IC.[224] Appreciable American attention to the connection between Islam and terrorism directed against the United States began soon after the al-Qaeda attacks of September 11, 2001. President George W. Bush appeared to link Islam in general to terrorism in his public comments, a view that offended people who saw most Muslims as peaceable people. Recognizing his misstep, Bush thereafter sharply distinguished Islam from Islamist terrorism. According to Muller, NCTC analysts generally viewed this perspective as reasonable and Bush was popular at NCTC.

The IC's views of terrorism changed appreciably, however, when Obama took office in 2009. Obama was much less concerned than Bush about terrorism, and he called Islam-motivated terrorism "violent

[223] Michael V. Hayden, *The Assault on Intelligence: American National Security in an Age of Lies* (New York: Penguin, 2018), 36-37, 196. See also Brennan, *Undaunted*, 269-271. Former national security advisor Lieutenant General H. R. McMaster wrote that when he was posted to Kabul in 2011, he forwarded to Washington a paper forecasting that a resurgent al-Qaeda in Iraq would defeat Iraqi security forces. In response, "senior intelligence officials" in Washington had a "tepid" response because the paper's "predictions did not conform to U.S. leaders' self-delusion" that the war was going well. See H.R. McMaster, *Battlegrounds: The Fight to Defend the Free World* (New York: Harper, 2020), 255.
[224] Author discussion with David Muller, July 11, 2019. Former CIA officials generally agree that Bush was well regarded at Langley. One former senior official told me that Bush was much more impressive in personal dealings with intelligence issues than in his official public appearances.

extremism," effectively denying the obvious fact that Islam motivated groups such as al-Qaeda. Even DNI Clapper, who bought Obama's diversity and inclusion agenda wholeheartedly, wrote that Obama refused to use the term "radical Islam."[225] Muller recounted an episode in which several CIA analysts talked to a group of about 100 people at an NCTC location, mainly NCTC analysts, using words that closely mimicked Obama White House language on terrorism[226] (future DCIA John Brennan was Obama's counterterrorism advisor at this time). Muller believed the NCTC group was overwhelmingly unimpressed by the CIA presentation. Several people in the audience asked pointed questions and expressed disagreement with the presenters.

Muller said that at about the same time as the CIA briefing, Javed A. was appointed to manage the NCTC office charged with overseeing and coordinating the counterterrorism intelligence training programs of all federal agencies. A practicing Muslim, Javed expressed pleasure about how he had excised Islam from training courses at the FBI, where he previously worked, and he said he planned to do the same in the ODNI and in the IC generally.[227] Javed went to Obama's National Security Council (NSC) staff after he left ODNI.

Muller noted the incongruity of Obama's and Javed's views of the Islamic world. Much of global terrorism was then (and remains) motivated by and/or justified by interpretations of the Koran. There would not have been an NCTC—which was created by the intelligence reform act of 2004, itself a product of the September 2001 attacks—if not for Islamist terrorism. Muller argued that removing Islam as an analytic variable in terrorism analyses was akin to discussing World War II and the Holocaust without assessing the influence of Nazi ideology and Adolf Hitler's *Mein Kampf* on Germany's foreign policy from 1933 to 1945. The IC might have accepted that the connection between Islam and terrorism is politically sensitive and been careful in wording its analyses, as Bush belatedly was, but it did not have to accept a near-ban on considering Islam when analyzing terrorism. Former FBI official William Gawthrop has

---

[225] Clapper, *Facts and Fears*, 336-337.
[226] Author discussion with David Muller, July 11, 2019.
[227] Ibid.

made similar points, observing that U.S. government officials have often been vulnerable to misrepresentations of Islam.[228]

Muller concluded that what he called Obama's Islamophilia eventually was largely accepted in the IC, creating a worldview-driven bias in analysis of an issue of national and global importance. In his last years in office, Obama proposed that the Census Bureau create a new minority group called MENA—for Middle East and North Africa—that would include people from the mainly Muslim countries from Morocco to Iran.[229] This move, not completed before he left office and then stopped by the Trump administration, would have defined another demographic group meriting the special preferences of identity politics. It presumably would have created another "affinity group" to which the IC would have had to cater, further balkanizing the workforce.

Obama's view of Islam affected organizational cultures as well as analysis; it both arose from and contributed to the associated idea that "diversity is a good thing," which played a major role in the IC outbursts in early 2017 against Trump's one-time proposal to restrict immigration from several predominantly Muslim countries.[230] This occurred even though the countries were hotbeds of terrorist activity and Islamist radical groups were then well known to use refugee flows to infiltrate fighters into target countries.[231] DCIA Brennan agreed with Obama in this arena, too. He told a reporter in 2017:

> Over the last couple years, we really tried to make a real effort to have the Muslims within the CIA workforce feel that they were as special and as valued and important as everyone else. Too often, there has been unfortunate rhetoric that has been the equivalent of

[228] William Gawthrop, *The Criminal Investigator-Intelligence Analyst's Handbook of Islam*, 1st ed. (Parker CO: Outskirts Press, 2021), especially 92-104.

[229] Mike Gonzales, *The Plot to Change America: How Identity Politics is Dividing the Land of the Free* (New York: Encounter, 2020), 77-94.

[230] Ed Lowther, "Election 2020: Trump's impact on immigration – in seven charts," BBC, October 21, 2020, https://www.bbc.com/news/election-us-2020-54638643.

[231] For example, Carl Anthony Wege, "The Changing Islamic State Intelligence Apparatus," *International Journal of Intelligence and CounterIntelligence* 31:2 (2018): 278.

Muslim-bashing. A lot of employees took that rather personally.[232]

This bias seems likely to have affected analysis and organizational culture over what has become an extended period of time. It seems to remain a factor, given that the ODNI, as evidenced by *The Dive* issue noted above, continues to tell intelligence officers generally to give kid glove treatment to Islam and to Muslims.

Political activism, including leaks

DEI is an ideology-based political agenda. Marxist orthodoxy calls for theory to be linked to practice. Obama and Biden, and their subordinates, have practiced critical race theory by employing DEI dogma to reshape the federal bureaucracy and instilled political activism in federal employees along with commitment to DEI principles. These, too, have had significant implications internally and on popular respect for the institutions of intelligence. Most obviously, DEI policies were a major cause of the unprecedented surge in political activism against candidate and then President Trump in 2016-2021. During the 2016 campaign season, Trump's promise to "drain the swamp" in Washington posed what many feds evidently considered to be such a direct threat to their beliefs and tangible interests that "defensive" action seemed necessary.

This politicization took time to build. Nicholas Dujmović observed that political discussions within the CIA during his later years there focused on core issues addressed by DEI policies.[233] Dujmović, who retired in 2016, wrote:

When I started at CIA in 1990, the organizational culture was such that one simply didn't express oneself politically, but I saw that gradually change over the decades to where it is both commonplace and, reflecting general trends in American society,

---

[232] Jenna McLaughlin, "More White, More Male, More Jesus: CIA Employees Fear Pompeo Is Quietly Killing the Agency's Diversity Mandate," *Foreign Policy*, September 7, 2017, https://foreignpolicy.com/2017/09/08/more-white-more-male-more-jesus-cia-employees-fear-pompeo-is-quietly-killing-the-agencys-diversity-mandate/.
[233] Dujmović conversation with author, June 2019.

decidedly left-liberal in nature, particularly on social issues dealing with sex, gender, and marriage.[234]

"Sex, gender, and marriage" are some of the arenas that DEI aims to influence. Combining Brennan's exhortation to employees actively to defend the DEI "progress" he engineered, comments of former employees such as Ned Price and Cindy Otis, information from leakers, and subtler information in many places, the evidence is strong that DEI policies and associated management emphasis played a major role in the outburst of activism against Trump, who DEI partisans legitimately feared might reverse the "progress."[235]

Another dysfunction that almost certainly occurred was that CIA analysts' "liberal biases" pushed publication of intelligence products on subjects President Trump was sensitive about, especially Russian meddling in American elections and assertions that only Russian meddling enabled his win in 2016."[236] Like all presidents, Trump had his biases and blind spots. But malevolently pushing this material amounted to political activism, not merely analytic bias. The CIA's intermittently used "truth to power" slogan reemerged in the Trump years as shorthand for the idea that intelligence officers know truth and that they can and should thrust their version of truth at Trump—a president whose policies and views they did not like.[237]

In a September 2020 leak, nine current and former CIA analysts complained to *Politico* that DCIA Haspel had cracked down on the volume of intelligence products on Russia going to the White House.[238] Although it is not uncommon for CIA and ODNI managers to shape the flow of intelligence products to the White House and NSC staff based on stated

---

[234] John A. Gentry, "An INS special forum: US intelligence officers' involvement in political activities in the Trump era," *Intelligence and National Security* 35:1 (2020): 6.

[235] For extensive treatment of this subject, see Gentry, *Neutering the CIA*, especially pages 118-199.

[236] Dustin Volz and Warren P. Stroubal, "Clash Quiets Spies," *Wall Street Journal*, July 6, 2020, A4.

[237] John A. Gentry, "'Truth' as a Tool of the Politicization of Intelligence," *International Journal of Intelligence and CounterIntelligence* 32:2 (2019): 217-247.

[238] Natasha Bertrand and Daniel Lippman, "CIA clamps down on flow of Russia intelligence to White House," *Politico*, September 23, 2020, https://www.politico.com/news/2020/09/23/cia-russia-intelligence-white-house-420351.

consumer preferences, and President Trump had made clear that he was sensitive about, and angered by, repetitive intelligence on Russian interference with American electoral processes, CIA analysts and evidently the staff that prepares the *President's Daily Brief* kept trying to bombard him with Russia stories. The leak suggested that the nine analysts believed they had a right to override agency management decisions and repeatedly thrust their version of truth at Trump, thereby further annoying Trump and undercutting Haspel's position with the president. In response, in 2019 Haspel reportedly asked CIA general counsel Courtney Elwood to review the work of "Russia House," a CIA element that works Russia-related issues, suggesting that she distrusted the objectivity of that unit's personnel, their products, and at least some normal agency product review processes.[239] Reportedly, Haspel accused Russia House analysts of repeatedly lying to her and in 2020 replaced the unit's head for undisclosed reasons.[240] These actions were unprecedented. Leakers unsurprisingly accused Haspel of trying to appease Trump.[241]

Perhaps relatedly, just before Trump left office in January 2021, the IC's analytic ombudsman, Barry Zulauf, wrote an unclassified report to the Senate Intelligence Committee in response to its questions about Russian and Chinese efforts to influence the 2020 U.S. elections.[242] Noting differences in views among unnamed IC analysts and ODNI officials on the issue, Zulauf said some China analysts "appeared reluctant to have their analyses on China brought forward because they tended to disagree with the Administration's policies, saying in effect, I don't want our intelligence to support those policies."[243] This constituted a violation of

---

[239] Ibid.

[240] Ibid.

[241] Ibid.

[242] Ellen Nakashima, "Political appointees, career analysts clashed over assessments of Russian, Chinese interference in 2020 election," *Washington Post*, January 8, 2021, https://www.washingtonpost.com/national-security/russia-china-election-interference-intelligence-assessment/2021/01/08/7dc844ce-5172-11eb-83e3-322644d82356_story .html.

[243] Julian E. Barnes, Charlie Savage, and Adam Goldman, "Trump Administration Politicized Some Intelligence on Foreign Election Influence, Report Finds," *New York Times*, January 8, 2021, https://www.nytimes.com/2021/01/08/us/politics/trump-administration-politicized-election-intelligence.html. Zulauf's letter to SSCI acting chairman and ranking member, January 6, 2021, page 3, is embedded.

IRTPA's Section 1019, which bans analyses slanted by political considerations, as well as ICD 203 "Analytic Standards" and long-standing IC cultural norms of apolitical public service.[244] Zulauf also said that senior ODNI officials, including DNI John Ratcliffe, did not adhere to established tradecraft standards in reporting Russian election interference in several reports in 2020. Perceptions of politicization threaten the "legitimacy" of the IC's work, Zulauf wrote. Trump's press critics unsurprisingly trumpeted only Zulauf's comments about Ratcliffe. Presumably because his memo irritated senior career intelligence officers, Zulauf soon thereafter was packed off to de facto exile as the intelligence representative at a prominent university.

Former CIA counterintelligence chief Mark Kelton observed that widespread worry within the CIA in 2015, when Brennan was director, about the "fraying professional discipline" of the workforce turned into a "tsunami" of leaks in the Trump years.[245] Brennan encouraged CIA employee activism, but currently employed intelligence officers cannot go on MSNBC or write op-eds in the *Washington Post*, like activist former intelligence officers did, leaving leaks their major avenue of activism. We know a bit about the magnitude of the surge in leaks. Then-Attorney General Jeff Sessions announced in August 2017 that the Justice Department received more criminal referrals from government agencies requesting investigations into unauthorized disclosures of classified information in the first half of 2017 (President Trump's first months in office) than in the previous three years combined.[246] Sessions provided few details but said the FBI had created a new counterintelligence unit to manage the cases. Senator Ron Johnson (R-WI), chair of the Senate Homeland Security and Governmental Affairs Committee, became concerned about leaks and had his staff look into the matter. Staffers found that in Trump's first 126 days in office—January 20 to May 25, 2017—

---

[244] ICD 203, third edition, December 2022, https://www.dni.gov/files/documents /ICD/ICD-203_TA_Analytic_Standards_21_Dec_2022.pdf.
[245] Mark Kelton, "Honoring the Oath Taken by Intelligence Officers Means More than Politics," *Cipher Brief*, February 26, 2024, https://www.thecipherbrief.com/column _article/honoring-the-oath-taken-by-intelligence-officers-means-more-than-politics.
[246] Del Quentin Wilber, "Sessions Promises Crackdown on Leaks," *Wall Street Journal*, August 5-6, 2017, A4.

125 leaks of national security information, as defined by Obama in an executive order issued in 2009, targeted the new administration.[247] This rate of almost one per day was seven times the rate of targeted leaks, identically defined, that Obama's administration faced in his first 126 days in office.[248]

Anecdotal evidence also points to a much higher volume of leaks. Michael Hayden's "journalist friends" told him in 2017 that "a lot of [intelligence] folks are certainly more willing to talk to them."[249] Former Deputy Director of Central Intelligence John McLaughlin told a television audience "so many people are coming out of the woodwork."[250] He incongruously added that he doubted many of them were intelligence people. In 2017, Clapper denied, wholly without credibility, that *any* intelligence people leak classified material.[251] Yet he admitted in his book that he himself had leaked.[252]

Reputational consequences

Intelligence officers' political activism and their tendency to throw Russia stories at Trump clearly annoyed the president, and surely has led many Republicans, especially, to be skeptical of CIA judgments.[253] A large number of articles and books have been published on the subject of the CIA "Deep State" and its alleged role in a purported coup plot against

---

[247] Kimberley Strassel, *Resistance: How Trump Haters Are Breaking America* (New York: Twelve, 2019), 73.

[248] Ibid.

[249] Hayden, *Assault on Intelligence,* 86.

[250] MSNBC, 2017, https://video.search.yahoo.com/search/video;_ylt=AwrBT9fV eiRZDtUAMklXNyoA;_ylu=X3oDMTEyNHY5aGhmBGNvbG8DYmYxBHBvcw MxBHZ0aWQDQjM1MTFfMQRzZWMDc2M-?p=%22John+McLaughlin%22+ and+MSNBC&fr=fp-comodo#id=24&vid=66440ec7e7adc0bf342d10e3656d0fb6& action=view.

[251] Gabrielle Levy, "Clapper Denies Intelligence Agencies Leaked Dirt on Trump," *U.S. News and World Report*, 12 January 2017, https://www.usnews.com/news /national-news/articles/2017-01-12/dni-clapper-intelligence-community-did-not-leak -damaging-dossier-on-donald-trump.

[252] Clapper, *Facts and Fears*, 231-232.

[253] For many examples, see Gentry, *Neutering the CIA*, 156, 224, 227, 248-250, 297, 388.

Trump.[254] Many of these were written by people who once respected the IC. Committees of the House of Representatives are at this writing still investigating the "weaponization" of the federal bureaucracy, an inquiry that prominently includes IC agencies.

The activism has generated polling that shows that Americans think increasingly poorly of intelligence, especially of the political activism of intelligence officers. While surely the IC's main clients, or "customers" in current parlance, are senior government decision-makers, the intelligence agencies rely on taxpayer funding and serve the public by improving national security-related decision making. Hence, the agencies have long sought both to inform citizens in general terms about a clandestine part of their government and to woo public opinion as an aid to furthering their interests.[255] An operational result of DEI-motivated political activism is falling public confidence in the trustworthiness of the agencies, which means diminished faith in the accuracy and integrity of the intelligence assessments that presidents and other senior decisionmakers use to make and rationalize their foreign policy judgments. [256] A Rasmussen poll released in October 2023 found that only 36% of American voters believed that intelligence agencies behaved in an impartial manner, while 51% said the agencies have their own political agendas.[257] Some 65% believed it likely that the agencies are influencing corporate media's coverage of political issues. Another Rasmussen poll released in March 2024 showed that most Americans believe the IC is trying to influence the 2024 presidential election.[258]

---

[254] For example, Jason Chaffetz, *The Deep State: How an Army of Bureaucrats Protected Barack Obama and Is Working to Destroy the Trump Agenda* (New York: Broadside, 2018).

[255] Christopher Moran, *Company Confessions: Secrets, Memoirs, and the CIA* (New York: Thomas Dunne, 2016).

[256] John A. Gentry, "U.S. Intelligence Deserves the Distrust It Is Generating," *American Thinker*, May 24, 2024, https://www.americanthinker.com/ articles/2024/05 /u_s_intelligence_deserves _the_distrust_it_is_generating.html.

[257] Rasmussen Reports, "Do U.S. Intelligence Agencies have Their Own Agenda?" October 3, 2023, ttps://www.rasmussenreports.com/public_content/politics/ biden_administration/ do_u_s_intelligence_agencies_have_their_own_agenda.

[258] Rasmussen Reports, "Election 2024: Many Voters Suspicious Toward Intelligence Agencies, March 7, 2024, https://www.rasmussenreports.com/public_content

This result is sharply inconsistent with the stated goals of many of the anti-Trump activist former intelligence officers of 2016-2021. Many of them rationalized their activism as an unfortunate necessity in response to Trump's purported "assault on intelligence."[259] They claimed they were only trying to defend the function and institutions they cared for deeply. But like many of their claims, hopes, and actions, this one has been both wrong and counterproductive.

This study also has further demonstrated that U.S. government partners of both the CIA and the FBI have also shown diminished confidence in their abilities due in significant part to DEI policies. The "National Alliance" of former FBI personnel cites details of a significant deterioration in the quality of special agents due to lower quality recruits and flawed personnel management, lower managerial expectations of recruits and agents, and management dishonesty about the nature of the problem.[260] As a result, there reportedly is widespread recognition by partner law enforcement agencies that FBI people, and thence the FBI as an organization, are less capable and more politicized than before DEI policies were enacted. We do not yet know the extent of lost confidence among international partners in U.S. intelligence agencies. But it seems likely that U.S. adversaries, including the intelligence services of Russia and China, which monitor U.S. politics and American intelligence agencies, are enjoying the spectacle of the slow-moving institutional suicide of important American national security-related organizations caused by DEI.

/politics/biden_administration/election_2024_many_voters_suspicious_toward_intelligence_agencies.
[259] Hayden, *The Assault on Intelligence*.
[260] Ibid.

Chapter 5

Conclusion

The evidence presented here strongly suggests that DEI policies have harmed national security. We can clearly observe and describe damage to processes and organizational cultures vital to national decision making and defense. The DEI policies of Presidents Obama and Biden, and many senior intelligence officials appointed by them, established practices designed to interfere with highly functional intelligence processes in ways that clearly cause procedural dysfunctions and sub-optimal operational results. President Trump largely kept these policies in place and only began to address them late in his administration. These results are not accidental. They are purposeful consequences of a domestically-focused ideological agenda designed to instill these changes permanently in the organizational cultures of IC agencies. At the same time, no evidence suggests that DEI policies enhance operational performance in the IC despite many such assertions. It is crystal clear that many IC personnel, including senior managers, recognize these problems but feel unable to oppose DEI policies without significant risk. The general public also recognizes problems with DEI policies: a June 2024 Rasmussen poll found that 29% of American adults thought DEI policies make companies better, while 38% thought DEI makes companies worse.[1] Many companies, institutions, and state governments are either reducing DEI policies and programs or abolishing them altogether, often citing their demonstrated ineffectiveness along with their fundamental unfairness as the reason.

The damage done to the IC by the Obama and Biden administrations has been significant. Trump's error was largely one of omission, not the

---

[1] Rassmussen, June 30, 2024, https://www.rasmussenreports.com/public_content /business/general_business/is_dei_causing_discrimination_nearly_half_think_so?ut m_campaign=RR06302024DN&utm_source=criticalimpact&utm_medium=email.

purposeful politicization of the Obama and Biden administrations, but the damage worsened on his watch because DEI became increasingly institutionalized without significant challenge and was also radicalized by the fact of his election. Trump and his advisors in 2024 seem to have realized that they made a mistake and reportedly have formulated plans to reform the bureaucracy if Trump wins the presidency again in 2024.[2]

While we can be confident that significant damage has occurred, we do not yet know what the eventual consequences of the damage will be. We do not yet know how badly senior decisionmakers have been misled by flawed data collection or DEI-colored analyses. Enemies have not yet attempted to exploit U.S. intelligence-related weaknesses and vulnerabilities in war or in other strategically significant ways. But perceptive adversaries surely have noticed at least some of the troubles identified herein and maybe others. They have probably reached similar conclusions about the performance of U.S. intelligence and will surely exploit what they see as major U.S. vulnerabilities at times of their choosing. Therefore, given the importance of intelligence to national security, we should conclude that DEI policies have already appreciably damaged national security. Given the history of Marxism in the United States as a tool of Soviet subversion, its role in developing DEI policies, and its transferal to anti-American actors at home and abroad, it is not far-fetched to believe the damage is intentional.[3]

We do not yet know enough about the damage because the agencies and their presidential masters have refused to examine the issue. More research on this subject is clearly warranted and has been highly productive in other areas of public life, especially including education and business. In the temporary absence of another major intelligence failure, Congressional oversight committees are probably the best immediate possibilities for meaningful investigations into the consequences for the agencies—and the nation—of DEI policies in the IC and the Defense Department. We may have to wait until the next big intelligence failure

---

[2] Will Weissert, "Trump wants to fire thousands of government workers. Liberals are planning to fight back if he wins," AP, February 16, 2024, https://apnews.com/article/biden-2024-government-regulations-democrats-6badc3b424b9eff3ba51e0ec35a8d824.

[3] Gentry, "Belated Success."

for a presidential commission to examine in detail the role(s) of DEI policies in causing the failure.

But awaiting needed details does not mean that addressing the issue should idle. To the contrary, DEI-related problems have been long in the making and will take much time to reverse. Time is of the essence.

President Biden and his intelligence appointees seem firmly committed to the ideology of DEI, as does his designated successor Kamala Harris, a minority woman who was chosen to be Biden's vice president on the basis of DEI gender and racial preferences. DEI principles form a core belief of their political party and command the allegiance of those who benefit from it holding office. Hence, it is unreasonable to hope that a Democratic administration will "see the light" and reverse policy, even if U.S. national interests are severely harmed. While Congress can and should act to hold the executive branch to account, the only real remedy will come from an administration that prioritizes reforming the federal bureaucracy, including the intelligence agencies, and removing DEI principles from intelligence and every other area of government.

Such a reform will face many challenges. Executive orders can be issued or changed easily, but some DEI-related policies have been institutionalized in laws that will have to be revised or reversed. Personnel management will be more difficult. At this writing, the intelligence agencies have been subjected to ideology-motivated institutional engineering for nearly 15 years, half a bureaucrat's working career. They are insular organizations. There are few political appointees at these agencies, meaning there are few senior leaders who have clout to order changes and reasonably expect that their orders will be carried out. New leaders will have to bring in new staff to help them or, better, identify serving officers of sound judgment to replace persons who have bought into the DEI agenda. Replacing rank-and-file career employees may prove a harder task and could be encumbered by legal issues. And of course, any leader seeking to remove DEI will encounter accusations of racism, sexism, ableism, homophobia, and other prejudices that are widely scorned.

Intelligence people, especially CIA officers, are adept at opposing would-be reformers who threaten their interests. As Trump's administration showed even without attempting a comprehensive reform, they will certainly resist through leaks and disinformation.[4] Future reformers can expect similar vilification and outright lies about them and their work. The only DCI who seriously attempted to reform the CIA, James Schlesinger for a few months in 1973 before President Richard Nixon made him Secretary of Defense, remains among the most unpopular CIA directors.[5] At the time, CIA security increased its efforts to protect both the man and his official portrait within CIA headquarters from irate CIA employees. A new generation of reformers who challenge the ideologies, interests, and psychological comfort zones of intelligence officers should expect similar abuse. The appearance of that abuse alone, however, will demonstrate conclusively the pressing need for radical reform of the U.S. intelligence community.

---

[4] Gentry, *Neutering the CIA*, 38-49, 231-328.
[5] Christopher Moran, "Nixon's Axe Man: CIA Director James R. Schlesinger," *Journal of American Studies* 53:1 (2019): 95-121.

Index

www.ingramcontent.com/pod-product-compliance
Lightning Source LLC
Chambersburg PA
CBHW072205270326
41930CB00011B/2539